MW00464201

Praise for *The Artist's Joy*

"The act of making music is in so many ways mystical but also highly practical. In *The Artist's Joy*, Merideth Hite Estevez has written a unique book, with calm and warm generosity, that is of relevance to all artists. I truly believe it will help us all retain our enjoyment of making music when the world and its events can seem so overwhelming and when challenges from our past may threaten to subsume our joy."

—**Nicholas Daniel**, international oboe soloist
and conductor, Officer of the Order
of the British Empire

"With clear writing and hard-won wisdom, Merideth Hite Estevez is the guide we need for a sustainable creative life. She knows the curves, pitfalls, and quiet gifts of the artist's path. This book is both a personalized toolbox and a well of deep universal insight for any artist feeling stuck, discouraged, or in need of fresh hope in their work."

—**Emily P. Freeman**, *Wall Street Journal* bestselling
author of *The Next Right Thing*

"This book provides several ways to unlock creative joy through inspiring stories and engaging exercises. By offering unique tools that awaken the senses and delight the inner child, Merideth Hite Estevez shows that it is not only possible to tap into your creativity, but that it is an essential part of life."

—**Tracee J. Glab**, executive director of
Flint Institute of Arts

"Merideth Hite Estevez's *The Artist's Joy* is a healing balm for the artist's soul. If you are seeking a spiritual companion to sustain a joyful, wholehearted creative life, look no further."

—**Ashley Hall-Tighe**, trumpeter for Canadian Brass, adjunct trumpet faculty at the University of Cincinnati College-Conservatory of Music, and certified life coach

"This fascinating, well-written road map on 'creative recovery' is not just for artists. Dr. Merideth Hite Estevez offers an incredible guide for anyone to find their inner artist. As she weaves in her remarkable story, Dr. Estevez taps into an essential truth about life: art can save the soul. In doing the work of healing herself, she's helping others—no matter their profession—find joy."

—**Kenneth Moton**, award-winning TV journalist, former network TV news anchor, and national correspondent

"What Dr. Merideth Hite Estevez is offering us within *The Artist's Joy* is both deeply tender and beautiful. Whether or not you consider yourself an artist, musician, author, or creative, she gently and lovingly guides us as readers to see anew how the gift of creativity is woven within each of our lives. I am truly grateful for this book and the spark it reignited within me to reconnect with the joy of creating in a way that offers wholehearted hope and healing."

—**Holly K. Oxhandler**, PhD, LMSW, associate dean for research at Baylor University's Garland School of Social Work, and author of *The Soul of the Helper: Seven Stages to Seeing the Sacredwithin Yourself So You Can See It in Others*

"Merideth Hite Estevez has done the artistic community a real solid with *The Artist's Joy*. In addition to her own innovations and helpful 'showing, not telling,' Estevez has collated the best arts insights from a trusted cast of characters, including C. S. Lewis, Madeleine L'Engle, and Julia Cameron. If you're looking for a book that can get you unstuck as an artist or fan into flame your already-bright spark, this is it. *The Artist's Joy* is, in short, an artful and wise gift ready-made for your toolbox."

—**Charlie Peacock**, Grammy Award–winning music producer and coauthor of *Why Everything That Doesn't Matter, Matters So Much*

"Merideth Hite Estevez has opened up her own story in a beautiful and compelling way, inspiring other artists toward their best work from a place of wellness and joy. What a gift! Brimming with touching stories, contemplative exercises, and self-coaching prompts, *The Artist's Joy* will usher any creative forward in their journey."

—**Katy Rose**, author and illustrator of *Lilibet the Brave*

"By the end of the prelude, you will know if this book is for you, and trust me, if you are an artist of any type, this is undoubtedly for you. Merideth Hite Estevez eloquently unpacks the urgency for joy, and then provides the tools for you to make yourself well. It's a journey you must take."

—**Quinn Simpson**, co-founder of Graydin

"*'If your creative practice costs you your joy in life, the cost is too great.'* Through autobiographical metaphors and stories of lived experiences, Merideth Hite Estevez offers a heartening message to creatives who suffer for and by their art. *The Artist's Joy* is more than a self-help book; rather, the reader is provided with thought-provoking questions that serve as motivational reminders that imposter syndrome, fear, and 'artist's block' are real, yet can be overcome through courage and self-forgiveness to find healing and joy."

—**Amy Hardison Tully**, DMA, Teresa Ann Carter King
Dean of the College of Fine Arts,
Texas Christian University

THE
ARTIST'S
JOY

THE ARTIST'S JOY

A Guide to Getting **UNSTUCK,** **EMBRACING** Imperfection, and Loving Your **CREATIVE LIFE**

Merideth Hite Estevez

BROADLEAF BOOKS
Minneapolis

Library of Congress Cataloging-in-Publication Data

Names: Estevez, Merideth Hite, author.
Title: The artist's joy : a guide to getting unstuck, embracing
    imperfection, and loving your creative life / Merideth Hite Estevez.
Description: Minneapolis : Broadleaf Books, [2024] | Includes
    bibliographical references and index.
Identifiers: LCCN 2023038121 (print) | LCCN 2023038122 (ebook) | ISBN
    9781506497242 (hardcover) | ISBN 9781506497259 (ebook)
Subjects: LCSH: Creative ability. | Creation (Literary, artistic, etc.) |
    Artists--Psychology.
Classification: LCC BF408 .E8738 2024 (print) | LCC BF408 (ebook) | DDC
    700.1/9--dc23/eng/20231205
LC record available at https://lccn.loc.gov/2023038121
LC ebook record available at https://lccn.loc.gov/2023038122

Cover image: shutterstock_2042438765
Cover design: Jamison Spittler

Print ISBN: 978-1-5064-9724-2
eBook ISBN: 978-1-5064-9725-9

Printed in China.

To Edwin, who helped me believe the truest things I know.
To Eva and Eli, the best things I will ever make.
And to you, reader, my "one." May you know you are worthy.

JJ

The discipline of creation, be it to paint, compose, write, is an effort toward wholeness.

—Madeleine L'Engle, *Walking on Water*

Contents

Part III: Recapitulation: The Theme Returns

Prelude
Break a Leg (or Don't)

"**I**'m fine."

"You have said 'I'm fine' five times in the last thirty minutes."

I stared at the carpet in Liz's office. She'd been my therapist since my first year at Juilliard. *God bless her.* I think. *I don't know how she does this all day.* I was very much not fine, but I wasn't ready to admit it. In truth, it would be years before I answered that question with any real integrity.

A graduate of Yale and a Fulbright Scholar, I'd gotten one of the coveted spots in the doctoral program at Juilliard. I was living in the greatest city in the world. On the outside, looking in, my life was *good*; I was more successful than I had ever been, and my career as a professional musician was about to take off.

I once heard the author Elizabeth Gilbert explain the difference between "good" and "well" in an interview. "There are a lot of things that this culture provides that will make you feel good. Lots of intoxicants, lots of sedatives, lots of distractions, lots of things to consume that will make you feel *good* . . . but that's not the same as feeling *well*." Besides the subtleties of grammar, there is a difference, isn't there? In some ways, feeling *good* is as simple as reaching for your phone. Feeling *well* is something else entirely.

To complicate matters, *being an artist* and feeling well are not two things that go together, historically: Van Gogh's ear. Mozart's entire champagne-soaked life. Beethoven's moods. I had a friend who quit after her first method-acting class at summer camp in high school because she felt, based on what the other kids shared, that there was simply not enough trauma in her childhood for her to be an actor.

I suppose what we all want to know is if creativity makes us crazy or if crazy makes us creative. Some studies explore how the arts and creative expression make us happy and healthy. "The Mappiness Project," a study from the early 2000s, measured the happiness level of certain activities and found that four of the top six happiest things we do are arts related. Numerous studies show how the arts lower cortisol levels, aid in healing, and create community. How can both things be true? The art is magical, and the artist miserable. The arts bring collective joy to society, but at what cost to those who create it? Two things are undeniable: many artists are struggling, and the tortured-artist trope is alive and well. I imagine if you have picked up this book, you know both to be true.

Anyone who has ever written a song or a poem after a breakup has felt the catharsis of creative expression. It is another kind of intoxicant. *Maybe we get addicted to melancholy because we have seen what creativity can do with it, how it takes the pain and makes it beautiful.* Maybe we get addicted to melancholy because we have seen what creativity can do with it, how it takes the pain and makes it beautiful. What do they say before the actor takes the stage? Break a leg. The spotlight is an exhilarating and risky place. And yet, our artistic practice turns even the most broken parts of ourselves into a mysterious mosaic of meaning.

But this is exactly why feeling well and being better than fine matters for the artist and for society at large. At its core, creativity is a generative, transformative, life-giving force for good in the artist's life. Making art can be a way we choose well-being, a tool to feel better, balanced, and more deeply connected to each other.

At its core, creativity is a generative, transformative, life-giving force for good in the artist's life. Making art can be a way we choose well-being, a tool to feel better, balanced, and more deeply connected to each other.

Ultimately, this book is about how to be well, be joyful, and be an artist at the same time.

ARTHUR

After New York City spit me out, I met Arthur. He was in one of my very first creative recovery groups. He only stopped talking while smoking, which he left to do about every eight minutes. He stood six foot three inches tall and probably weighed less than a hundred pounds. The fact that he had no teeth didn't stop him from smiling. He would come around for a few weeks and then disappear for months. Knowing more about mental illness now, I see these were likely signs of bipolar disorder, yet Arthur's life was a mystery to me. What I did know was that when he was with us, he lit up the room.

A friend of Arthur's said he had an off-the-charts IQ. I wasn't surprised. Once we got to talking about the science of light, he reminded me of what I had learned in school; that we perceive color by whatever an object reflects, even though all the colors of light are present. (For example, the cover of the book looks blue because when light hits, it reflects blue and absorbs red and green.) Arthur would attempt to master color while painting at the local shelter that provided art supplies and studio space for homeless artists. He would come to our group with four or five pieces that he wanted to show us, many of which were still wet. Each painting felt like the contents of his mind poured out on canvas.

Once, Arthur noticed me admiring one of his biggest, most colorful pieces. It was a wave in a cerulean ocean, the water reflecting a chartreuse sun with a foreboding red-sky backdrop. It was tumultuous and exuberant, terrifying and joyful, peaceful and chaotic—just like Arthur. He watched me looking at it for a whole minute before he said, "Sometimes this is the only certain thing. You swim when you go under. You try to see the whole thing as beautiful, even when it's scary as hell."

"What's the title of this one?" I asked.

His answer crashed into me.

"It Is Well With My Soul."

Just like the light reflecting off the blue book contains more colors than blue, just like Arthur is more than the sum of his highs and lows, just because you create art out of your pain does not mean you are your pain.

You are more than a diagnosis or neurosis, more than the sum of your failures or successes. I learned from Arthur that creativity can help us recover our joy, even when life's waves threaten to take us under. The wave painting made me want to stop letting the malaise and melancholy of my artist life be my entire personality, to stop letting them be the only color I reflect.

Joy is a feeling with all the colors in it.

Joy is a feeling with all the colors in it.

It can feel like bliss, but it is also deeply grounded. It includes grief *and* gratitude, pain *and* belonging. It's got the tears from laughter and loss.

Arthur knew all about that; I could see it in his painting, in his cloudy, yellow eyes. I'm so grateful to him for teaching me that art can be us seeking well-being in real time; it can be our recovery.

Creative joy means practicing saying, "it is well with my soul," without having to pretend there are no waves.

WHO IS THIS BOOK FOR?

This book is your companion on the path toward well-being and resonant joy in your creative life. A guide for how to live in a world that writes you off as blue because your work is blue. It is for all my fellow feelings-surfers out there.

For the ones who lost their joy in their craft along the journey.

It's for that moment when you feel the impossible weight of the rest of your artist life on your shoulders and when you cannot remember why you're even doing the creative thing anymore.

For the one who isn't even sure if they get to call themselves an artist. (Spoiler alert: they do.)

This book is for all the little moments you may or may not be noticing when you are most disconnected from the little kid who liked picking out songs on the piano or always asked for art supplies for Christmas.

For the one who gave up after one acting class.

For the one whom rejection or criticism threatens to defeat.

For the one whose mind is a toxic work environment.

Maybe instead of joy, you feel overwhelming dread and fear, muted disappointment, anger, or ambivalence, and you are wondering how creativity can help.

Or maybe you're like me and got to the end of twelve years of conservatory training at some of the best music schools in the world and couldn't even bring yourself to listen to music, much less play it.

This book is for you, for *us*.

WHY JOY?

There's something better than fine, better than saccharine sweet or shallow *good*: a well-being feeling with the whole spectrum of colors in it, something I call joy. And what I learned on my journey back to joy for music, what I'll teach you in this book, is that we find joy by living in congruence with what matters most to us, with what we believe to be true, with who we already are at our core. We can stop the negative inner chatter from taking us under, we can rebound from rejections and create inspired art from a place of deep resonance and even bliss. We can do more than fester in the pain that art makes meaningful. We can find a sustainable creative practice that doesn't burn us out or make us sick. Joy is something we can learn to practice receiving, and this book will be your guide on that journey.

Joy is a state of synchronicity of all the parts of yourself: your body, heart, mind, and spirit, your connection to yourself and others, and your connection to something larger than yourself. It includes well-being, but it does not require you to stop being who you are. In fact, finding joy feels like the opposite of self-abandonment or denial; it is a homecoming, a theme returning in the original key, but we will get to that.

WHAT CREATIVE RECOVERY LOOKS LIKE

In 2017, I started working with other drained artists who had lost their joy in their work. We met weekly to discuss Julia Cameron's seminal text, *The Artist's Way: A Spiritual Path to Higher Creativity*. The book is a potent tool, urging aspiring and working artists to recover their creativity by removing blocks and finding a sacred circle of community. It is also one of the top-selling self-help books of all time.

During that first Creative Cluster, I connected deeply with Arthur and others—a mosaic artist, an actor, one woman who called herself an "artist of life," and a spoken-word poet. It amazed me how much we had in common. Even though they weren't entrenched in the discipline of classical music, I saw how the creative impulse in all of us was calling out to be healed and seen, a thread that wanted to be picked up and reconnected somehow.

And so, we kept meeting, even after the twelve weeks of the book were over. We invited friends. The group became groups. At one point, I led a cluster specifically for artists struggling with substance abuse and behavioral health disorders. I called in a licensed art therapist to help me. Week after week, I felt something changing in me; I watched others change, too. I got certified as a creativity coach and started meeting one-on-one with people. I designed workshops around these topics to help artists find well-being and thrive, and the most amazing thing happened: the work began to heal me, too.

Since Arthur, I have witnessed thousands of artists' creative journeys toward joy. Their stories are woven throughout this book; in most cases, their names and details have been changed or combined to protect their identities. Stories are my memory of events, and I relate them in good faith with occasional creative license used to bring the stories to life. While I am a Doctor of Musical Arts, I am not a medical one. Nor am I a social worker. This book does not replace the need for therapy, medication, or Alcoholics Anonymous. (However, I have seen it make a great companion to your work with other forms of help.) Think of it as a message in a bottle from a fellow artist working to be well, here to share whatever tools I have found on my journey to joy.

I have developed and collected personal development exercises called "Études," a French word meaning *study*. Some are inspired by the treasure trove of personal development coaches and thought leaders I consumed during my own recovery, and others were developed with my coaching clients. They are designed to be returned to often, like musical études, which help those who practice them grow strength and facility in a particular skill. Get a special journal and set it apart just for the études so you can have the answers in one place. They will build on one another. You can also find a printable journal for each étude at artistsforjoy.org/book.

The work of creative recovery and creative well-being will increase your inspiration and even your productivity, but not in ways you may think or expect. Over the years, I have met all kinds of people from various artistic disciplines—across mediums, genres, age groups, demographics, faith expressions, and socioeconomic statuses. The walls of my home are covered with watercolors and acrylics, a mosaic, and a woven tapestry; works of art gifted to me by some of my beloved creative recovery friends. I also know of books, blogs, and music written by our community. That's the thing about artists: they tend to heal out loud, which is a wonder to witness. But what I find even more beautiful than anything they could ever make is watching them experience the joy of coming home to who they truly are, loving and accepting themselves, and believing they are whole.

HOW TO READ THIS BOOK

This book is organized into three sections: Exposition, Development, and Recapitulation, after the common three-part form you often find in classical music sonatas and symphonies. (By the way, while the book does explore many musical metaphors, it isn't just for musicians.)

As all forms do, sonata or symphony form charts the evolution of the theme in a piece of music—the motif and all the different iterations in which it appears. The form of this book represents the path we can walk as artists, which begins within, develops as we encounter the world, and returns to us, changed when we consider the ways creativity connects us to one another and something larger than ourselves.

In part I, the chapters and études will help you recover your child-like joy, move from disconnection with your physical body to compassionate embodiment, and more. This part will connect you to yourself in preparation for when your creative work meets the world. Part II will move you from isolation to connection, scarcity to abundance, and help you face any obstacles with grace, resilience, and sustainability. Finally, in part III, the Recapitulation (the moment in the musical form where the theme finally returns), the chapters and études move you from fear to courage, from bitterness to forgiveness, teaching a deep personal worthiness that will serve you in the face of any creative block.

If I could, I would make the music come from the pages of this text like one of those incessant birthday cards. The next best thing is a playlist or two. At the opening of each chapter, I have listed a track from "The Artist's Joy" playlist that goes along with the text from that section. Sometimes it's a piece I reference directly; other times, it is music from my first album that encapsulates the text's emotion. If you scan the QR code or follow the link in the back of the book, I will also take you to more music from my award-winning podcast. It is perfect to listen to while journaling, writing, painting, or while you're busy creating a life.

After the main text of the chapter, the self-coaching questions invite you to open up to yourself in your journal, a trusted friend, or a therapist. Then, the étude helps you practice what you've learned. Each chapter ends with True Things that can be used as mantras or affirmations, and I've left space for you to write more. The Coda, the extra added bit at the end, offers one more metaphor to consider.

Read the chapters in order, or skip around. A searchable index with topics and common creative blocks is also in the back for quick reference. Use the Creative Cluster Guide in the back to share your journey with friends and fellow creatives in your community. Start your own creative recovery group. This work changed my life.

THE HIGHER-POWER ELEPHANT

Most cultures have some type of creation story. I think that's because people have looked at the world and sensed its wonder; they have experienced the power of creativity themselves and long to explain it. The "aha" moments, the creative genius, the mysterious muse, and even basic enthusiasm (which comes from the word meaning "from the gods," by the way) are examples of how we keep reaching for spiritual words in creative conversations. I believe this is because being an artist means standing on the precipice of something mystical.

For the purposes of this book, spirituality need not necessarily mean religion. It means that to some, but not all. To me, the word *spiritual* signifies anything concerning internal experience, from your inner dialogue or mindset to what you believe to be true about the nature of the universe. In my groups over the years, I have seen artists from completely different sides of the religious/spiritual spectrum speak honestly about these topics without judgment, using their artistry as a common ground to stand on. Their openness has helped me expand my own vocabulary, and I hope the diversity and inclusiveness of these relationships come through in this book to meet you wherever you are. I have greatly benefited from naming the source of creative inspiration as something outside of myself, and I call that force Spirit or God. These topics will come up, and I hope you will see the discussion as an invitation. Claim your creation and creativity story and state the words you use for the creative force, whether you believe it is within or without. Regardless of your faith, background, or tradition, this naming and reflecting are valuable tools for creative recovery. I hope you will take what is helpful, follow anything that leads you to more freedom and joy, and leave the rest.

Arthur's wave painting sits above my desk as I write this. One day he disappeared from the group and never came back. I hope he is somewhere taking his meds, diving headfirst into life, running around town with wet paintings, working toward feeling *well*, riding the wave.

Becoming well is not always simple or easy, but it is joyful. I believe that joy comes as the result of many tiny choices, the whole of which is greater than the sum of its parts. By seeking joy and all of the colors it contains, we become integrated, aligned versions of ourselves, and we create from an overflowing fullness even when tempted to objectify and glorify our suffering. We ride any wave we face, even if we are pulled under.

> *I believe that joy comes as the result of many tiny choices, the whole of which is greater than the sum of its parts.*

We build a creative life that is sustainable and resonant. Our art becomes a type of flotation device, a way to become more fully ourselves, way past fine.

May it be so with Arthur. May it be so with you.

PART ONE

Exposition
The Opening Theme

Ex·po·si·tion, /ˌekspəˈziSH(ə)n/

1. A setting forth of a meaning or purpose.
2. The part of a movement, especially in sonata form, in which the principal themes are first presented.

If you want to work on your art, work on your life.
— Attributed to Anton Chekhov

Introduction to Part I
Life Is a Symphony

Joy is a dusty old library. It is thinking of your life as a work of art. For the purposes of this paragraph, imagine it as a symphony, a thick musical score on a shelf in the back of some cavernous structure full of books. You have the call number and find the volume, pulling it down onto a nearby table. It is almost too heavy to lift with one hand. The typography of the title page has serifs that feel old and new at the same time. You continue turning, the page thick with its antique finish, and see it: the immensely intricate, immaculately designed score. The perfectly ordained order of things, the twirls, squiggles of treble clefs and staccato markings, the thrill of trill and gruppetto; it's all there, just as you sensed it would be.

You take your finger and follow each measure, beginning at the key and time signatures. Like a ballerina on pointe, the music leaps from the page. The sound comes to life in your mind's ear. You know what *A thread of bright yellow in a tapestry of crimson.* you are looking for and immediately recognize it: the opening theme, the first motif that characterizes the whole thing. A thread of bright yellow in a tapestry of crimson. Which instrument plays it? The violins (like many Mozart symphonies)? The cellos (like Beethoven's

Eroica)? What does it sound like? Noble? Buoyant? Impassioned?

In this part, we will start with the opening theme of you. Exploring our connection to the inner artist-child within each of us, we will learn how to stay tethered to that deep sense of self in our creative work. We will examine how taking care of ourselves, physically and emotionally, is the bass note to a joyful, creative life. Then, we will develop a sustainable artistic routine, learning to find lasting change and set inspiring goals one note at a time.

ONE

Ode to the Inner Artist-Child
Being Imperfectly Whole

"Moderato: Coda," from *Appalachian Spring*, by Aaron Copland (1944)

The wound is the place the Light enters you.

—Rumi

ALEX

At our third meeting, she admitted that the only time she wasn't thinking about using heroin was when she was making mosaics. I didn't know the details back then, but anyone who saw her knew she had a rough life. Her eyes were barely open. From the smell of her, through her veins ran pure tobacco. She was part of one of the first classes I ever facilitated on creative recovery. I'd never been friends with someone like her before.

In the class, we all spoke vulnerably about our connection to making art and our identity as artists. Unlike many of the others in the class, myself included, who were struggling with things like writer's block or burnout, Alex's art *was* her recovery. It was keeping her clean; it was keeping her alive. She made the mosaics out of broken glass she collected on the streets, mixing the cement herself in a local mission that provided studio space for homeless artists. She loved to show me how raw the work made her hands, like a badge of honor.

Using broken things to craft massive, intricate designs, she made discards beautiful, whole. It was then that I started believing that art is a gateway drug of its own. One that heals us.

TERMINAL

It was 2013, and I was standing on the corner of West 65th Street and Broadway in heels, static cling making the regalia stick to my legs, the elastic on the graduation cap stretched tight around my big head, my shiny new Juilliard diploma in hand. Decades of practicing and performing, years of dissertation writing, had brought me to this moment. Smiling for Dad's camera phone, I wondered: "How am I going to do this for the rest of my life when I don't even like music anymore?"

On the first day of the rest of my artist life—the moment that all the sacrifice and discipline had been for—my cup was empty. I had received my terminal degree in music from the apex of music institutions in America. *Terminal* was the perfect word because something in me had died.

I had received my terminal degree in music from the apex of music institutions in America. Terminal was the perfect word because something in me had died.

Julia Cameron says, "Discipline is like a battery, useful but short-lived." And, boy, was I the Energizer bunny. That camera at my graduation caught the exact moment my battery died. And what fuel did that battery run on?

PERFECTIONISM

The need to be perfect was a one-hundred-pound bowling ball chained to my ankle. If you struggle with it, you know the crippling need for things to be just so. I would repeatedly play the same measure until my wrist was numb. Even when my friends or colleagues applauded me, I would lie awake at night obsessively replaying everything I had "done wrong" until every ounce of joy from a performance was gone. Perfectionism made it impossible for me to be happy, even though my life on the outside looked like I had achieved everything I had dreamed of.

Are you unable to put down the pen, close the computer, clean the brushes, or let something stand as finished? Can you enjoy going to concerts, or are you just sitting there listening for mistakes? Do you fixate on the one thing you did wrong instead of rejoicing in the many things you did right? Or maybe your perfectionism is so debilitating you can't even get started. Do you spend two hours on tasks that take others mere minutes?

Perfectionism is particularly insidious for the artist because it often disguises itself as excellence or even humility. It can seem to come from an honorable place; high standards are not a bad thing. In Western culture, we make an idol out of excellence and perfection. For these reasons, no one really knew what a toxic place my own mind really was back then. Not even me.

Don't get me wrong, it is not the desire to be good or the dream of creating something beautiful or even excellent that's the problem. The problem is that behind my perfectionism was egotism, judgmentalism, and pride. Behind that Energizer-bunny discipline was a tired, scared, insecure girl, deathly afraid of failure. No

wonder I hated music. I hadn't spent any time cultivating my joy for it. Instead, I had devoted twelve years
of college working hard from a place of fear. I was my
own taskmaster and enough was finally enough.

THE ARTIST-CHILD

If my love of music died on West 65th Street that day
in May, it was born in 1995 in a small bedroom in
rural South Carolina. I was twelve and had somehow
acquired my very own CD player. For the first time in
my life, I could control what I wanted to hear and no
longer had to wait for the song to come on the radio.
(The music I liked never came on the radio anyway.)

The psychologist Carl Jung is often the one credited
with developing the idea of the inner child archetype.
Psychologists use this lens to help us understand our
behaviors, to explain who we are now in light of our
memories of our childhood selves.

My own real-life artist-child insisted on wearing
leotards to school. She hosted a morning radio show on
her karaoke machine about middle school gossip. She
would wait until she was alone in the house and sing
show tunes at the top of her lungs in front of the family
room mirror. Her prized possession was a multidisc set
of the works of Aaron Copland. She listened to the coda
of *Appalachian Spring* so many times that, amazingly,
her sister in the next room didn't kill her. She was brave
and expressive, tender, and ready. When I think about
her with her thick glasses and wispy hair, I want to hug
her, but she rarely stops moving long enough for that.

Something about music, the Copland coda, contained
a whole world to her: the strings, the flute, the simple
harmonies. They called to something pure, peaceful,

and true. She wasn't listening for it to be perfect; she was listening because she was desperate to understand what made it glow. She had only just begun playing oboe then, but she just had to play that music, to live inside of it, to embody it. Her love of organized sound was born from a bottomless curiosity and a certain something that I might now call hope. To borrow a phrase from Ann Patchett, that music was her "getaway car," and she couldn't wait to jump in and speed right out of town.

THE PRICE OF PERFECT

When I think about the kid lying on her bedroom floor with her eyes closed, listening to Copland, I see almost no connection between her and the Doctor of Musical Arts standing on the street, wondering how to go on. The kid with the CD player was curious, creative, and experimental, attempting to play Copland's notes on her brand-new rented oboe. The newly minted Doctor of Musical Arts in 2013 was a product of hard work, nitpicking performance, and kicking herself for missing a single note. Perfectionism can steal the joy at every stage in the creative process. Some clients struggle to get started for fear of making a mistake, others find themselves stuck in the middle, paralyzed with fear in the face of even a routine setback. For me, it was always hardest in hindsight. I would stare into the dark hall during the applause, internally calling them liars. Even in the face of success, all I could see was how I could have been better.

Have you compared your artist-child to your adult self lately?

Perfectionism was such a hard habit to break because it was so effective at helping me get ahead, which is just what my ego wanted. Being unhappy unless things were perfect, berating myself if I didn't get up early, practice longer, obsess about every detail—I believed this was how I got into Juilliard in the first place. I had to maintain that perfection level because I worried I was nothing without it. I was exhausted, but didn't know who I was without the discipline battery firing on all cylinders.

You can't talk about perfectionism without also talking about shame because they are two sides of the same toxic coin. Or, as Brené Brown says, "When perfectionism is driving us, shame is always riding shotgun, and fear is the backseat driver." I needed to be perfect because something deep inside me believed I wasn't good/talented/thin/smart enough. Every lesson, concert, audition, and exam was a test of my worthiness, of whether I could hack it, whether or not I was an imposter, and whether or not I belonged. I realize now that I practiced and achieved not from a place of joy and curiosity like the girl playing Copland's coda on repeat. I practiced to avoid failure, afraid of what it would mean about me—what would happen to me—if I didn't succeed.

It wasn't entirely my fault. This shame-based pedagogy is used throughout many arts institutions to this day. We're pressured to work hard and achieve because we're warned of the consequences of failure. Professors and schools of art and music could inspire students with the call to create beauty or to serve some common good. They could use carrots, some wield sticks. No wonder we get burnt out; no wonder the batteries die. Few teach how to recharge them. It's unsustainable to create from a place of needing to be perfect, to prove somebody wrong, or to outrun our shame. When we stop for even a second, shame rushes in, proving the mentors right.

> *It's unsustainable to create from a place of needing to be perfect, to prove somebody wrong, or to outrun our shame.*

Joy is a balm for the wounds of shame pedagogy and perfectionism; its seed is already inside each of us. The end goal of joy is authenticity and sustainability, it is curiosity and delight, not winning or being the best.

Because here's the thing the little girl listening to Copland knew, the thing that the Energizer-bunny-Juilliard-grad would come to realize years later: the antidote to perfectionism is not working harder; it's vulnerability; it's returning to yourself and being that person.

There comes the point where holding in whatever you long to create—where keeping inside your chest the song you want to sing—hurts more than any shame you might encounter when it comes out imperfectly. There comes the point where you can't hold it in anymore, where you have to write, sing, play, and create.

It's a common misconception that perfectionism makes us great. In fact, it is one of the greatest road-blocks to productivity and progress. To find a joyful, creative life, I've faced the push and pull of vulnerability and perfection, realizing that letting go of one means fully embracing the other. I've seen how the safety of silence ran against the longing to release the song I knew I was born to sing. Opening up, being vulnerable, led to my finding a creative life that resonated with joy. I left the safety of silence and the promises of perfectionism and chose vulnerability. I chose to return to my inner artist-child.

Five years after that day on West 65th Street, it was a mosaic artist and recovering heroin addict who taught me the power of imperfection, the freedom and purity found in making things you care about. She showed me how, in the face of fear, to steer right into vulnerability and let the light shine through any brokenness and woundedness.

Alex's goal was never perfection. She was not interested in that. Her goal was release, focus, effort, to follow the purest child-like impulse to get her hands dirty. The making of mosaics was her lifeline, and she helped me remember how music was once my lifeline—my hope, too. The answer to perfectionism is not more hard work. On the contrary, it's sinking into vulnerability,

The answer to perfectionism is not more hard work. On the contrary, it's sinking into vulnerability, disconnecting your sense of worthiness from the quality of your work.

disconnecting your sense of worthiness from the quality of your work. It is remembering your inner artist-child, helping her heal if she needs it, and letting her lead you again.

Out of principle, Alex never sold a single piece of her art. I didn't understand why at the time, but I get it now. She wasn't looking to monetize or quantify the value of her expression, of her healing. There was so much light in her mosaics. The brokenness of things is where the growth starts, where the resurrection happens, and where the healing is. Within it, there is a creative flow that can sustain us instead of draining us. We just have to be willing to show up to the stage, canvas, or blinking cursor, even when we are terrified of being wrong. What we create may be imperfect and vulnerable, but in the end, it'll be something better. It will be real.

I thought my creativity had died at the hands of perfectionistic discipline, but once I stopped trying to be perfect, I started finding joy in music again. Returning to the music I loved as a child, dreaming up musical projects around what mattered most to me, and sharing my struggles with other artists in creative recovery groups led the way to joy.

Just like Alex's mosaics are not for sale, allow me to remind you of the same: your value is not in success or some approval from the world. Say what you'd say regardless of who will listen, and lean into the fear and vulnerability of the moment, because when you feel that, it means joy is close at hand. Let your imperfections give you information about what you value, where you should go next, and what you are learning. Return to the inner artist-child, tend to her, love her, forgive her.

Do not be afraid. In everything you make, look for the light trying to get in through the broken pieces, making them imperfectly whole. Follow its courage through the cracks and out into the world. When the getaway car pulls up, climb in.

SELF-COACHING QUESTIONS

Answer these questions in your journal or out loud to a friend or therapist.

1. What did you like most about yourself as a child?

2. If not perfectionism, what creative blocks, internal and external, separate you from child-like joy?

3. List five things you would do if you weren't afraid of failure.

4. When was the last time you felt creative joy?

5. Who in your life can you come to when you feel shame?

ÉTUDE: WORD-MOSAIC: IMPERFECTLY WHOLE

Open a journal to a clean page (or an 8.5 × 11 sheet of paper works, too). Starting somewhere in the middle of the page, write adjectives, images, and memories that describe yourself as a child. Write them in no particular order but in present tense. They can be simple words or phrases, memories, or physical descriptors. Avoid writing in lines or groups; sprinkle these words about your inner child all over the page. If you need help remembering, reach out to someone that knew you as a child or return to pictures or videos.

Now, on the same page, in another color ink, add words for yourself today. What are you like now as an adult? What visuals encapsulate you? How do you spend your time? What things do you love? Write them around whatever space is left around the inner-child words.

Reading through both lists, what do you notice? Draw lines to things that are still true, connected, or otherwise related. Put stars by things from your childhood that are not present in some form in your adult life. Where can these pieces of yourself fit into your life today? Are they still needed? Is there anything here asking to be attended to, healed, or revisited? This is who you are. Let this word-mosaic teach you whatever you need to learn today.

May it show you the beauty found in accepting all that you are. It isn't perfect. And when we love ourselves in the midst of the vulnerability that creativity requires, we begin to feel something better than perfect. We begin to feel whole.

Write a couple of sentences of reflection after this exercise, perhaps as a letter to yourself as a child or a letter from your inner child to yourself today. What do you want your inner artist-child to know? What would your child self like to say to you? To anyone else in your memory?

Example:

free	busy, full life	
always singing	giggles while she is learning	
always thinking	wispy strawberry blonde	
rich brown hair, some grays		loves kombucha
loves chips	loves learning	oboist
thick glasses	Lasik surgery	

CODA ⊕

The Berlin Wall was more than 110 miles long and 12 feet high. It was built with brick at first and eventually included concrete and steel. It was called the "Wall of Shame" or *Schandmauer* by many in the West because it represented the lack of freedom and the disunity of postwar Germany.

Do you know what they did with all the demolished concrete, steel, and other materials once the wall was torn down? Did they sink it to the bottom of a lake? Did they hide it somewhere in hopes of pretending it never happened? You likely have seen some pieces sold or gifted to museums worldwide, including Israel, South Africa, and America.

Here's the thing that's interesting to me: the rest of the wall—the parts no one wanted as paraphernalia, what I imagine were the ugliest parts—were used to build new roads in Germany. They took the "Wall of Shame" and recycled it into roads. Roads for everyone. They laid it to rest right under their feet. They used it to rebuild the city. As Rumi reminds us, the wound can be an opening for the light to shine through the brokenness beyond us.

How will you recycle your shame? It won't be perfect—it can't be, just by the nature of its materials—and what a relief! When you are ready, because it may not happen immediately, what roads will you build with the remnants of your pain?

Five True Things (the last one is yours to add):

1. Perfectionism does not make me more productive.

2. Being real is better than being perfect.

3. Inside every artist, there is a child longing to be loved.

4. Shame is not a sustainable tool for motivation.

5.

TWO

Ode to Self-Care

The Creative Instrument Is You

"Summertime," from *Porgy and Bess*, by George Gershwin, featuring Ella Fitzgerald

The only reason for mastering technique is to make sure the body does not prevent the soul from expressing itself.
— La Meri, *Dance Has Many Faces*

NIKKI

The reviews called her voice honeyed and effortless. In reality, it took a lot of effort in the form of a finely tuned vocal-health regime: ice chips, followed by warm water with lemon, no caffeine, dairy, or alcohol, no tomatoes or spicy food (they have too much acid). She consumes one-half of her body weight in ounces of water daily.

This seems like a big sacrifice to me, but then she opens her mouth to sing "Somewhere over the Rainbow" or "Summertime," and the feathers of the song envelop me, and I'm ready to rid the whole world of caffeine and alcohol and spice if I could keep hearing that.

I asked her once how she had found her way to this way of life, if her teachers taught her, or if she'd come up with this herself through trial and error. All it took was a bout of muscle tension dysphonia to make her realize how fragile the voice really is. Muscle tension dysphonia is, in simple terms, when the muscle that controls the voice box becomes tense. It causes one to lose voice control and is most common with singers under high stress.

When Nikki's mom died of cancer, Nikki got a terrible cold. Her voice was taking so long to recover that she decided to see a doctor. "They told me it's a stress reaction. That the grief had caused the miscoordination of my voice box." She went on vocal rest for three months. She grieved her mother the best way she knew how, and during that time, she wondered if she'd ever sing again.

Even if your instrument doesn't reside in the center of your throat, caring for and loving your body is an act of creative recovery.

HUNGRY

As I collect more and more stories of artists who struggle, I see how issues with eating and food are typical. Clients have shared how much energy they expend daily thinking about calories in and calories out, only to finish a stressful project and binge eat. Actors and dancers feel pressure to maintain their weight as they age, even after pregnancy or a major injury. They feel despair and jealousy when they compare themselves to someone skinnier in the same production. A violin soloist skips lunch to fit into the dress and decides to "drink dinner" post-performance. Restriction, binging, excessive exercise, dangerous body-image goals, and unrealistic beauty standards leave many artists sick and sad.

My own "body management strategy" involved extreme calorie restriction, constant dieting, and exercise, all fueled by anxiety and a deep underlying hatred for my body. How I managed to exert so much energy practicing while eating only 600 calories daily for five years, I'll never fully know. Just like my perfectionism for music, my disordered eating made me feel better and worse at the same time. The constant judgment took many forms, like the pair of size two jeans that were too tight to wear out of the house that I would make myself try on every few days to confirm I could still button them. If I couldn't, I'd go into a spiral of self-hatred that would undoubtedly involve skipping dinner. Being thin felt so good because it was something I could control. I could count the number of pretzels and assure myself that two tablespoons of peanut butter was dinner, drinking a teaspoon of coconut oil to fend off hunger. I'd go on long runs and drink coffee all day, switching to wine in the afternoon. I would punish myself for all the ways I had "failed" in my lesson or rehearsal by working through dinner. And on days when things had gone well, I would allow myself an actual meal in celebration. Then I repeated the cycle the next day when I woke up and had gained a pound.

I took out all my perfectionism-fueled rage on the very thing that was holding me upright. My "healthy" lifestyle and newly slim physique were often commented on by friends, family, and complete strangers. No one seemed to notice or care that the state of my body was a result of hatred, not joy.

In one picture from that time, my eyes look vacant, like the joy behind them had been lost along with the water weight. All I can remember is how insecure I felt, how ugly and gross. I remember how many times I had changed my clothes before leaving the house and the sour mood that had ensued when the extra small top was tight in the armpits. That girl took up less space compared to this body I'm in now, and the smaller I got, the bigger the lies I told myself and didn't believe. Just get thin enough and reach that arbitrary number on the scale (which, by the way, changed when each goal weight was met); getting there would mean finding joy. Then, I would feel better, successful, and worthy. At my thinnest, I was still within the "healthy" range for my short stature, which is why no one truly noticed how I was harming myself. Years later, I realized there was no secret number on the scale or small enough clothing that would help me love myself. Instead, my disordered eating had drained me of my energy, literally and spiritually.

Luckily, while the field of instrumental classical music has its body-image expectations (as many careers do), I never experienced anything like my friend Julia, a modern dancer and choreographer who, in college, overheard her ballet teachers talking about her, calling her big. This was one reason she had left ballet and found herself now as a modern dancer, even though her first love was dancing *en pointe*. Even though she was making peace with her body more and more as she aged, she still felt the need to exercise on her day off in order to "earn" a shower.

Loving your body is an act of creative recovery because we cannot separate our creative impulse from its physical expression in the form of a human body on this Earth. It does not matter if you are a dancer whose arms are their instrument or a writer or painter who rarely graces a stage; your inner artist lives inside a *body*, and that body deserves love, showers, and fuel.

It does not matter if you are a dancer whose arms are their instrument or a writer or painter who rarely graces a stage; your inner artist lives inside a body, and that body deserves love, showers, and fuel.

In Julia Cameron's book *The Artist's Way*, a creative recovery guide, she says, "treating myself like a precious object, makes me strong." I remember after I left New York, reading that, feeling skeptical. I had believed that the thing that would make me strong was restriction and breaking a sweat. But now I know: if the inner artist is a child, everyone knows children respond better to kindness over harshness any day. Discipline and withholding can get results temporarily, making this type of behavior so addictive. You truly feel in control, but as with all discipline motivated by shame instead of joy, the battery eventually runs out. It stops working. You get hungry again, physically and spiritually, and thank goodness you do because when our bodies communicate, we need to listen.

Dedicating your life to this process, being a conduit for creative flow, in the service of making art, takes so much effort and energy. Finding the river of creative inspiration and then hating your body in the process is like sinking your boat. There is no creative joy without befriending yourself and making peace with the body that holds you, your creative impulse, and your very being. Perhaps this is what the quote (often attributed to playwright Anton Chekhov) means: "If you want to work on your art, work on your life." Treating ourselves like precious objects requires us to watch with wonder as our body seeks to partner with us and to listen better for what it needs, to become resilient to the shameful messages of what shape or size we should be, to love ourselves.

Some readers over the years have taken issue with treating yourself like an object. They shared that it feels like the very definition of objectification. And so, if that terminology is triggering for you, please feel free to change it to something you feel depicts your intimate relationship with your body. For me, this idea resonates because my body is a precious object that houses, but is also separate from, my identity. When I make my body my identity, I am tempted to take all the anger and perfectionism I feel for myself and try to change my outward appearance. The self-coaching questions will help you create your own phrase or body-positive messaging that encourages self-love and compassion.

My disordered eating never got as dangerous for me as it is for many others. Some might say what I experienced was the norm, but however common these types of thought patterns are for women *and* men, I refuse to call them normal. Finding a good therapist and leaving a few toxic relationships helped me recover the most. Even now, years later, I remember those feelings of isolation. Very few people in my life knew how I channeled my anxiety into an obsession about every single ounce I gained, every calorie I consumed, how the fear of gaining it back would follow me like a shadow, how I had made my body my enemy. My body and I are still working on our relationship.

THE FIRST COACHING QUESTION I ASK

When I am coaching a new client, they often come into the session eager to explore the presenting creative issue—the procrastination or the writer's block, for example. But the first question I ask is: What did you have for lunch today?

I try hard to slow them down, to remind them creative practice exists in a creative being, that is, a physical body. Of course, it matters what you ate for lunch. Little things matter; your body and its needs matter.

I know that loving your body can feel like a pipe dream. Perhaps it royally failed you, betrayed you, and left you wondering if it seriously has it out for you. I can imagine our culture or maybe even real-life human beings have been saying you haven't earned your shower, or you are so talented but just "too big for ballet," not behind your back, but right to your face. You believe deep down, even subconsciously, that it isn't ok to take up space, to be you. When you don't fit into the ideals of this toxic image-conscious world, you feel worthless, othered, and less-than. Is it your skin, your nose, or your uterus? Maybe you've spent thousands of dollars on plastic surgery or hair removal services, and no matter what you do, you can't outrun the deep shame, disappointment, injustice, and pain in your body. Maybe your body is the scene of a crime where very real violence against you has taken place. And, of course, the trauma keeps you stuck. You read my words about loving your body and ask yourself: How could I?

Whatever your story, you are not alone. There are resources for even the deepest of wounds, and whenever you are ready to begin the process of healing, it is not too late. I have worked with artists whose bodies have suffered unspeakable things. And I have watched with my own two eyes their recovery. The language of self-compassion can sound like a foreign tongue, but we can all learn it with the right team of guides, therapists, doctors, and truly compassionate loved ones. Perhaps

The language of self-compassion can sound like a foreign tongue, but we can all learn it with the right team of guides, therapists, doctors, and truly compassionate loved ones. Perhaps most powerfully, I have seen how the arts can be the rope we use to climb out of these pits of despair and self-hatred; we can create our way back to healing and acceptance.

most powerfully, I have seen how the arts can be the rope we use to climb out of these pits of despair and self-hatred; we can create our way back to healing and acceptance.

Author Sarah Bessey names the key difference between self-care and self-comfort. "Self-comfort numbs us, weakens us, hides us; it can be a soporific. But self-care awakens us, strengthens us, and emboldens us to rise." What would it look like for you, at eighteen or seventy-eight, to choose self-care over self-comfort? To make peace with your body? To invest in its healing and flourishing, to treat yourself like the precious miracle you are—today, right now, this moment—regardless of your jeans size, scars, or stretch marks? What would it look like to treat this body of yours with the respect it deserves, to see it as a container within which your eternally beautiful and precious Self resides? Artists can see the beauty in precious objects better than anyone can.

THE PROBLEM UNDER THE PROBLEM

Because here's the truth: you are the creative instrument. Even if you aren't a singer like Nikki, your body and mind are the vehicles that are using the brush or writing the chapter; if there is no *you* there, then there is no art. The container of your creative impulse—that's your body; that's you. And that body will keep recruiting whatever unsuspecting muscle, unhealthy self-comforting behavior, or coping mechanism it needs to get you what your powerful mind requires. We can't keep denying the fact that the pain or the disordered eating are just symptoms. The real problem is deeper. The real problem is that we work too long without rest, or we do not feel worthy. The real problem is the abusive relationship or substance abuse. The real problem is the grief.

Nikki's voice box tightened up and stopped functioning because she'd lost the person who meant the most to her in the world. Her soul was grieving and so was her body; it recruited every possible muscle to carry the brunt of that impact, and in the end, it had to go for the jugular. And we lose our mothers, don't we? We have things that happen to us that try to break us, and then we look down and wonder why we're broken. The work she had to do to sing the role was nothing compared to the recovery and process of grief. But the pain of being human needn't stop us from creating forever, and it won't when we allow ourselves to heal, when we give ourselves fuel, when we stop white knuckling our way through the pain, and love ourselves instead.

In the end, Nikki went on vocal rest and worked with her doctors and voice teachers to find a vocal regime that works for her. She healed. The loss of her mother is not something she will ever fully get over, but now singing has become an outlet for expression again, an active way to grieve. Treating yourself like a precious object looks different for everyone. You must name that for yourself. For me, intense restriction was being used for punishment and shame, while for Nikki, her vocal regimen (which includes plenty of restrictions) comes from a place of deep care for herself. For both of us, though, it looks like loving the body we are in, right now, today. And sometimes, that will hurt more before it feels better. It often means asking for help. This is the only body you get. It holds all the creative offerings you have within it. It is calling out for your love and respect, will you answer?

The renowned choreographer La Meri invites us to believe that technique and regime exist to clear the path for the body to express all that the soul longs to say. Taking care of yourself means working to understand how your body works, listening deeply to what it needs, because the instrument is *you*.

So, what's for lunch?

SELF-COACHING QUESTIONS

1. What is your relationship with your body like now? Where would you like it to be?

2. What spoken and unspoken beliefs do those in your art form or community hold about what a body should look like? Can you think of examples of people acting outside these prescribed norms?

3. How do you feel when you read: "Treating myself like a precious object makes me strong?" What other words or phrases communicate self-compassion and shame resilience? Write a few mantras for yourself and notice which ones are easier to believe than others.

4. What do you seek out of self-comfort? Self-care?

5. Who in your life do you know and trust that you can share body shame with?

ÉTUDE: CHECKING IN WITH YOURSELF

Develop a ritual of checking in with your body. Sit in a posture that allows you to pause for a moment.

You could sit in your chair and put your hand on your heart, close your eyes while you sit in the sun or get into your favorite yoga pose. (One client does it every time she washes her hands, pausing to look at herself in the mirror.)

Whatever you decide, stop moving for a moment and turn your ear toward your physical body. Ask your body, "What do you need?"

Check in with your muscle groups, your joints, your skin, your hair, and nails; be inside your body.

Take some deep breaths.

Notice what you are physically feeling. Left shoulder tight? Eyes a little dry? Tired legs?

Listen and notice everything your body is saying.

However your body feels, whatever your body needs, listen intently like a friend would.

How can you provide for your body's needs?

BUILD YOUR SELF-CARE TEAM

Use your études journal to answer the questions below. Share your responses with a friend or therapist.

What appointments do you need to make? Check off each one after you schedule it. Taking care of your health is not self-indulgent. It is the ground in which the seeds of joy are planted.

When you are at the appointment, book the next one, even if it is a year or more out. You can always reschedule, but having it on the calendar keeps it front of mind.

- Annual check-up with your primary care physician with blood work
- Therapy/behavioral health
- Reproductive health
- Dermatology
- Dentist
- Mammogram, colonoscopy, or other screenings
- Ophthalmologist
- Nutritionist
- Physical therapist
- Chiropractor
- Massage therapy
- Hair
- Nails
- Aesthetician
- Counselor
- Sponsor
- Spiritual director
- Coach
- Others? Write them in your journal

(Talk to your doctor about what is right for you.)

I need _____ hours of sleep to feel rested. Lately, I've been getting _____ hours.
I drink _____ servings of coffee or caffeinated beverages per day.
I move my body _____ times per week.

What kinds of clothes make you feel like your best, most confident self? (If you're not sure, ask a stylish friend to take you shopping to explore different styles.) Clean out your closet of clothes associated with body shame and sadness.

Describe your alcohol use. How many drinks do you have per day/week?

How many times per day/week do you use illegal drugs?

OK, what is the real number? In case you lied to the questions above, write the real answer in your journal.

Could you stop? Do you ever lie or hide drinking or using?

Do you practice behaviors that are destructive to your health? If so, you're not alone. Find a recovery group through Alcoholics Anonymous, Eating Disorders Anonymous, Drug Addicts Anonymous, et cetera. Most have daily online meetings. Do not believe the lie that you need the addiction to be creative. You can't create anything if you're dead. Recovery is possible.

CODA ⊕

When it comes to what things look like, we here in the Western world (in case you haven't noticed) are obsessed with perfection, meaning symmetry and ideal proportions. This aesthetic goes back to the ancient Greeks, who were obsessed with completeness and perfection in everything from math to ethics, architecture, and of course, art. It made a comeback in the Renaissance, and some argue it never left.

In ancient Japan, however, it was *imperfection* they valued. *Wabi-sabi* is an aesthetic that values impermanence and incompleteness, reminding us of the unique beauty and value of things we find in nature that are never perfect (by Plato's standards, anyway.) *Wabi-sabi* can look rustic, simple, and even rough to our eyes. In *kintsugi*, the art of repairing cracks in pottery with gold dust, brokenness is celebrated and valued, and imperfections are not something to be hidden but to illuminate.

What would it be like to see your body—including your scars and other painful or shame-inducing places—what would it be like to see your brokenness repaired in gold, deemed precious, valued, and wonderfully made? There is an entire worldview where there is wisdom and beauty in the marks experience leaves, in the memories of what living can do to us.

What would it be like to see your body—including your scars and other painful or shame-inducing places—what would it be like to see your brokenness repaired in gold, deemed precious, valued, and wonderfully made?

And we don't have to go to ancient Japan to live that way, we can do it now, naming our bodies as beautiful, accepting them in each moment, becoming resilient to shame, and claiming the power of *wabi-sabi* for ourselves. A brave, creative life can leave a mark. May you be stronger at the broken places, see them etched in gold.

Five True Things (the last one is yours to add):

1. Learning how to take care of myself takes work.

2. Sometimes self-care can feel painful.

3. I do not have to earn my shower.

4. Studies show that those who eat more fruits and vegetables are less likely to experience symptoms of depression.

5.

THREE

Ode to Creative Routine

Practice as a Spiritual Practice

"Au Loin," *Chant for English Horn and Piano*, Op. 20, by Charles Koechlin

Attention is the beginning of devotion.

—Mary Oliver, *Devotions*

WILL

Will invited everyone from our creative recovery group to an installation of his latest sculpture project. One chilly spring morning, we huddled around the fountain he'd help restore in a city park. Will seemed a bit nervous. His eyes darted back and forth between us and the fountain. He had remade parts of it from scratch, replacing figures that had deteriorated beyond repair.

At the Q&A, I couldn't resist asking what I had been wondering since we met.

"How do you learn to do that? Create such detailed figures out of stone?"

"My work as a sculptor starts each day the same way. Many times, in this very park, I come, find a comfortable spot to sit, grab my sketchbook and draw from life."

"What does that mean, *draw from life?*"

He grinned and quipped back, "Draw what I see. Translate the space between me and the world. Take something living and breathing and make it a two-dimensional proof of life. This daily routine of devoting myself to seeing and sketching, stretching my eye muscles to see up close and far away, up close and far away, over and over . . . that is the almost spiritual work that must happen before I pick up a tool to sculpt anything. Taking in everything all at once, each tiny line, each blade of grass, each shadow and shape, is like seeing through a dirty mirror, slowly wiping it clean. There's a sense that the form is already within the materials; it is only a matter of subtracting what is not needed. Sculpting happens only after sitting quietly and seeing what is already there."

Will reminded me that all sustainable and joyful creative routines are not just acts of discipline but devotion.

ENERGY MANAGEMENT

I used to have this quote posted in my office at my first university teaching job. It's by author Annie Dillard:

> How we spend our days is, of course, how we spend our lives. What we do with this hour, and that one, is what we are doing. A schedule defends from chaos and whim. It is a net for catching days. It is a scaffolding on which a worker can stand and labor with both hands at sections of time. A schedule is a mock-up of reason and order—willed, faked, and so brought into being;

it is a peace and a haven set into the wreck of time; it is a lifeboat on which you find yourself, decades later, still living.

Many things in this quote resonate with me. Who doesn't need a lifeboat in this chaotically creative life? The truth is, I have been known to worship my schedules. I remember planning out every hour of the day in college and following through with it. But at times, to a fault—hello, anxiety. Managing my schedule like this was like I had a button that I could push to send my nervous system into overdrive, a discipline button.

Paul Graham, a computer scientist, had something else to say about schedules in his 2009 article. As a computer programmer, he noticed how he and his colleagues worked with a different type of energy than other tech-team members. He labeled this maker versus manager energy: The world's most powerful people work with manager schedules, scheduling meetings every hour to get things done. Makers, on the other hand, need larger swaths of time without interruption. Graham says, "A single meeting can blow a whole afternoon by breaking it into two pieces, each too small to do anything hard in."

Life as an artist is the work of energy management. We need schedules, yes, Annie Dillard is right, but we need unscheduled time to explore, play, dream, and tinker. The purpose of the schedule should be to help us get things done while protecting our maker energy at all costs. The world is trying to make us managers, and if we aren't careful, that schedule lifeboat we're floating on could end up being the creative block itself, a tool for distraction and procrastination.

Life as an artist is the work of energy management.

I think energy management is particularly difficult for entrepreneurial artists. For example, my creative work doesn't always require me to be in a maker state of mind. Creativity coaching and teaching workshops are two very creative things that require the energy of leadership and detail orientation, not to mention time management. They are manager energy, but part of my creative life, nonetheless.

My maker energy schedule when I was back in school went like this: a 45-minute warm-up routine I did before my 8:00 a.m. ear-training class. I didn't realize it then, but that was sometimes all the maker time I got in a packed manager's schedule. The door to the big conservatory building would click open at 7:00 a.m., and I'd be waiting there most mornings in the dark, with my pick of practice rooms. I left the overheads off. The bright green light of the metronome clicked methodically, and the tuner's loud drone gave me a reference. I'd go through the steps. Starting with a slow ascending pattern, tuning every interval, making it fit as best as I could in its spot, the half step hovering in the air like a ballerina's arm. I would attempt over and over to make these patterns effortless, seared in my muscles' memory. I never played music before 8:00 a.m., just fundamentals, which is its own kind of music. There are only seven unique notes in the Western classical major scales; most mornings, seven felt like plenty. In those early morning sessions in the dark, I found my voice, started making the oboe an extension of my own.

THE GOOD NEWS

In many religious traditions, like Hinduism, devotion involves locating your soul in relation to the divinity. The Latin word "devotion" comes from the same word for "vow" and the root of the word "consecrate," so devotion also denotes promising something, setting it apart for a special purpose. We are showing up as an act of discipline and commitment but also as an act of naming our location.

Having grown up in the Protestant Christian tradition, devotional time was just another thing to check off the schedule. Read my Bible, check. Prayed, check. So, in all those years of hearing the word "devotion," I never stopped to realize that I had been doing this daily in the practice room for decades.

It confirms for me that this whole thing we do, this showing up at 7:00 a.m. to play long tones, waking up in the middle of the night with the idea, choosing to believe we have something to say even when we are faced with rejection or disappointment— the artist's life is a spiritual one. Mary Oliver tells us "Attention is the beginning of devotion," and so we must constantly ask, "What am I paying attention to? Artists are creatures of devotion, revelation, and faith. The Manager loves discipline and the Maker devotion. Practice is a spiritual practice.

Artists are creatures of devotion, revelation, and faith.

Looking back on it, I know now that the devotion to the early morning warm-up routine changed my skill level and my soul's balance. It became a thin place where something mysterious and beautiful could be found at the shape of the next scale or in the resonance of the perfect fifth when it was really in tune. It was where I was able to tell myself the truth. To hear the truth in the metronome and the tuner drone. Finally, a true north to follow, blend into, lean against. Some mornings it was—and is—easier than others. It's the repetition, the showing up, that makes it holy and life-giving.

Isn't it good news that at the center of music, at the bottom fundamental of it, it isn't exclusive or *who's better* or *winning* or *perfect*? You don't have to make up the beats per minute or the long tone pitches that resonate in overtones. It is all already in there; you are invited to harmonize with it. You aren't a servant to it either; its vibrations are sympathetic. The overtones are always ringing, inviting you to sing or play along.

The overtones are always ringing, inviting you to sing or play along.

Yet, like religious devotion, when we show up for artistic devotion with the wrong intentions—if we are doing it to feel superior, to be a martyr, to prove to ourselves and everyone else that we are *good*—that puts the ego center stage, not the object of our devotion. And that's why the early morning fundamentals practice was unsustainable for me back then. That scared and insecure girl in college who worshiped her schedules was waking up before everyone else to practice because it made her feel slightly less anxious and because her teacher told her to.

Practicing with devotion rather than discipline is about mindset, approaching the fundamentals with surrender and awe, and resting in the knowledge that A-440 hertz (that's the frequency that most orchestras and pianos are tuned to) isn't going anywhere. Practicing with devotion is practicing with reverence. When I approach this habit with reverence and devotion instead of duty and superiority, it becomes joyful again.

DEVOTION WITH DISCIPLINE

Protecting the maker energy with devotion is something each artist has to do for themselves. It is one of the single most important tools, after taking care of oneself, that we must learn.

Mind you, most of this book was written in the early hours before the sun rose. I still feel most like a maker in the morning. But any book that tells you there is only one way or time of day to be creative was written by a manager.

Maybe you have small children who keep you up all night, so mornings are a nonstarter. Maybe you have a nine to five that leaves you zapped, and the only time you can find is one hour during lunch to sneak across campus to the music department piano practice rooms. Maybe you're dealing with a chronic illness or grief that makes it hard for you to plan. There are seasons of life when you feel like you're drowning, and the idea of cultivating a creative routine feels like reaching for a chocolate truffle when what you really need is a square meal.

Being a maker in a manager world means being disciplined about devotion and joy. It means finding your own way, in whatever season you are, to carve out some uninterrupted maker time—a routine of joy—like a master sculptor. Joy is not a delicacy that only healthy, rested, together people get. When we engage creatively with a spirit of devotion instead of discipline, we satisfy a deeper hunger. We "feed the lake," as Madeleine L'Engle says, contributing to a pool of meaning both beyond and within ourselves.

Just as in religious devotion, what if our fundamental practice reminded us of all that is beautiful and sturdy about our art form? What if it helped us locate ourselves in space and time? To see our practice as collaboration and meditation on something already spinning, seeing what is already there? We then could subtract the ego, the false self, and the needing to be great, like Will would carve or whittle away in sculpture making.

You may be thinking, *Where am I going to find this kind of time?* Resist the temptation to say you have none. Think of creativity like hunger: a basic human need or urge you get to satisfy no matter how busy you are taking care of people or doing your day job. Joy is not a delicacy, it's a byproduct of wholehearted living.

Creating in the cracks is still creating.

Yes, large swaths of time are best, whole days or half days of maker energy are, of course, great. But I would say just forty-five or even twenty minutes of maker time every day is better than quietly wasting away in a manager's life. Creating in the cracks is still creating.

The coaching questions and étude for this chapter will help you zero in on a routine that works for you; however, there are some fundamentals here: Resist the temptation to plan too much inside the actual practice time. Just know that whatever small chunk of time you can give to practice with devotion will serve your creative impulse trifold. It resonates far beyond whatever time you can find. Do not get discouraged or impatient when there isn't much product to show for it yet and resist the temptation to measure by what your schedule produces—that's your manager talking. That is not the point of practicing with devotion. The maker knows all about devotion; exploring the fundamental is never time wasted. After you craft your routine in this chapter, in chapter 5, we will discuss how crafting the right goals can reduce overwhelm and help you progress through small steps.

When you practice your art form through a devotional lens, you may feel freer, more open, and more connected to your artistic voice. You may find yourself getting stronger, sounding better, feeling more skilled—but those are just byproducts of the real goal, the real purpose: devotion. Let your schedule be a lifeboat, then, not a straitjacket. Practicing this way locates us in relation to our maker selves; it reminds us that we needn't reinvent life but draw from it; creative devotion makes everything shimmer with abundance, peace, and divinity of all things.

SELF-COACHING QUESTIONS

1. Does anything about your artistic practice feel like a spiritual experience now? If not, what does it feel like to you? *Yes, all of it.*

2. What currently motivates you to practice? Shame? Fear? Joy? Curiosity?

3. Do you have a "discipline button"? How do you get yourself to do things?

4. How might you be benefiting from staying in the practice rut?

5. Who do you call upon for support when you feel unmotivated? *Marian, Debra, Gayle M*

ÉTUDE: BUILD A CREATIVE DEVOTION ROUTINE

Use the following questions and prompts to develop a routine of creative devotion that works for your life season.

1. What is at the core of your art? How could you break it down to the simplest of skills or reflexes? Examples could include music = scales or long tones; writing = free

journaling, haikus; theater/dance = physical movement/ stretching. These are just ideas, there is not one answer.

2. What makes you feel most nimble, relaxed, prepared, and ready to get down to work creatively?

3. What kind of time do you have to give to the above in this season? What kind of energy do you have to give? When can you carve out time?

4. What sounds fun? What feels like playing?

5. What obstacles get in your way? What can you do *now* that will make showing up easier *later*?

6. Craft a simple ritual you can implement today based on your responses. Choose a time at the best time of the day. (I highly recommend mornings, but if that's a no-go, try during the mid-afternoon slump or right before bed.) Set a timer if that helps. Make it so simple that it does not require much thought. Learning to create in the cracks of life will forge a deep connection between your inner artist-child and your everyday self.

Example of a creative devotion routine (from a children's book illustrator):

"I will hand-letter one of my 'Five True Things' for fifteen or twenty minutes after I make coffee, but before I unload the dishwasher. I will leave my materials out the night before for ease and display the finished project to encourage me."

Try to do the routine for five days in a row. After five days, ask yourself: What is working? What isn't? How do I feel? If you encounter resistance, revisit the answers to the questions above.

Creating in the cracks can feel frustrating, and transitioning in and out of the devotion routine might initially feel bumpy. Design an "on-ramp," a simple ritual like lighting a candle or saying a prayer before you begin. An "exit ramp" also helps; make your favorite beverage when you're done or stand up and stretch for a few moments before moving on to the next thing.

In the end, it all comes down to showing up. Remember, the goal is not necessarily to write the next Great American Novel with this routine but to forge a new relationship between you and your creative impulse. It will involve sacrifice, but this practice should make you feel better, not worse. If it doesn't give you a jolt of joy, shift the routine somehow until you find something that works for you.

CODA ⊕

Composer and organist Johann Sebastian Bach's compositional output included over one thousand pieces of music. People don't often realize that Bach occasionally used other composer' styles, melodies, and ideas in his work. His mind was like a sponge, absorbing styles from Italian composers like Corelli and Vivaldi. He reimagined others' music, folk melodies, Lutheran hymns, and more. What we hear as one-of-a-kind genius was, in truth, a potpourri of many geniuses threaded through the mind of one more.

At the end of each of his compositions, Bach would sign his initials, JSB, followed by three other letters SDG, which stood for the Latin phrase *Soli Deo Gloria* or *to God alone the glory*. Another lesser-known fact that is often told today is that he put another acronym at the beginning of each of his compositions. JJ or JH, *Jesu Juva* or *Jesu Hilfe*, which means, *Jesus help*.

Radical Amazement

What if you aren't doing this thing alone? What if we don't have to approach the practice room or a writing desk as the gauntlet where—by our own strength—we must make something great? What if there is help to be found and someone to ask? Who has come before you that sends their love and support as you create, who has passed down their canon, melody, and style almost as a love letter? Maybe Jesus is that someone. Or maybe it is a sibling or trusted mentor. The point is: we are not alone.

Remember: your job is to carry the flag, not reinvent it. Instead of trying so hard and needing to win, publish, or achieve, maybe the purpose is to use your creative process as a spiritual GPS, locating you in space and leaving proof that you were here. Your creative process is a vessel through which a force flows, instead of the force itself.

I believe Bach knew this. He gave God the glory, but he also asked Jesus for help. When we approach our creative impulse as an invitation to devotion we can release duty, martyrdom, ego, and pride. Imagine, a thousand works of art later, being as joyful as ever.

Five True Things (the last one is yours to add):

1. Time is finite. Energy grows or diminishes. Manage "maker energy" first.

2. "Showing up is the first step to creating a different reality" (Marianne Williamson).

3. "A journey of a thousand miles begins with a single step" (Chinese proverb).

4. Creating in the cracks is still creating.

5. _Being an artist is not a lonely struggle. I am in a partnership with God._

THE ARTIST'S JOY

FOUR

Ode to Ear-Training
Hear All Your Life Is Saying

"Sarabande," from *Cello Suite in E-Flat Major*, BWV 1010,
by J. S. Bach

Before you tell your life what you intend to do with it, listen
for what it intends to do with you.
> —Parker Palmer, *Let Your Life Speak:*
> *Listening for the Voice of Vocation*

MIA

The disclaimers poured out from the minute she arrived at our creative recovery group. "I'm not an artist. I'm not talented. I am not blocked, per se; just curious about what you're doing here, saw your ad online. Don't mind me; I'm no artist." She finally let the secret loose a few weeks in. She whispered like it was explicit: "I sing," she muttered, "in my car."

Mia's father had told her she didn't have a good voice when she was a kid and her brothers made fun of her too. She had learned early on not to sing where anyone could hear. Now as an adult, she'd strap herself into her car, close the sunroof and the windows, wait for the back roads where she knew she was alone, and then she'd open up her voice, like one of those velvet-lined boxes full of breakables. She belted the words to songs she could never forget. Turning up the stereo so loud, she couldn't even hear herself.

Singing in her car was when she felt the freest. A default mode; quieted mind, meditative breath, but not in a life-avoiding kind of way. In fact, more than once on the other side of that singing, she had found epiphany: One drizzly night, she pulled into her driveway after a long commute, having sung through tears, she finally realized what she wanted to do, what she had to do. She sang what she couldn't say. She knew after that drive she had to end her marriage.

Creativity is an invitation to listen to our lives.

EAR-TRAINING

First thing in the morning every weekday, students of the freshmen class of the conservatory experience a rite of passage: the jolting repetition of clunky harmonies and meandering rhythms played over and over at the crack of 8:00 a.m., usually in a basement. It is its own type of wake-up call.

Ear-training classes made me wonder if learning music was just busy work, picking apart melodies and chords and categorizing them, but for what? I also always seemed to be searching for a pencil; you were never allowed to write on music in ink. From the first day, though, I could hear Mozart's joy, Beethoven's passion, and Bach's piety. *Teach me what makes them sound like that*, I remember thinking.

One University of Chicago study says one in ten thousand people have perfect pitch, the natural ability to recognize and identify pitch out of thin air;

that is .01%. Somehow, twelve were in my freshman ear-training class. I had all my key signatures memorized and knew how to analyze basic music, but I was not one of the twelve with magical ears. I was envious, of course, and frustrated. I remember wondering if my ears were even trainable, until Yale School of Music, until Panetti. It was Dr. Joan Panetti who showed me how Bach could turn a theme inside out in a single-voiced cello suite. Panetti brought me to the center of the music.

Panetti wouldn't dare call what she was teaching "Ear Training." How basic. Instead, it was "Hearing." She wouldn't just train my ears, she would teach me to *hear*.

Instead of a small classroom in the school's basement, Panetti would gather all the first-year students into the large concert hall. (It was still at 8:00 a.m., but no matter.) Hearing always began with experiencing music live. If the piece required a large orchestration, *we* would be the performers, singing through an entire symphony or requiem as a class—vocal majors and nonvocal majors alike. We started inside the score, and this was how I learned to hear.

Through learning to hear, just as I expected, just as I had sensed as a child, I found a holy place.

Suddenly, the pages of part-writing practice, the highlighting of each seventh chord and its resolution—analyzing the composer's every pen stroke—served a greater purpose: to show me that Mozart's exuberance and Beethoven's fire were all a result of seemingly simple choices that worked in tandem to create a complex kaleidoscope of sound. The miracle was there for the hearing.

When I catch the tail end of Brahms's *Requiem* or J. S. Bach's *Magnificat* on the radio, I remember singing in that hall, my oboe-player voice wobbly, feverishly turning the well-worn pages of my white binder, the energy Panetti brought into the classroom, into life. My musical knowledge was a drawstring, and hearing pulled it together. Just as there was a difference between knowing about music and truly *hearing* it, listening to our lives requires us to develop a different kind of ear.

WHAT KEEPS US FROM HEARING

Ironically, the more adept I became at understanding music, the deafer I became to hearing my own inner song. The noise of other expectations and some implausible definitions of success still keep me from hearing the truth of who I am.

In *Let Your Life Speak,* Parker Palmer wrote, "Before you tell your life what you intend to do with it, listen for what it intends to do with you." How many artists leave school with ears sensitive to harmony and eyes masters of color theory, yet remain unable to discern who they are or where they should go next? Many people in my creative recovery groups show up asking big questions or are considering a career change. A pesky dread or inexplicable lack of fulfillment keeps them awake at night.

I wish the answers were as simple as opening the score, that there was an earthly guide as patient as Panetti to help us hear our lives. While we don't always have those tools to understand life's greatest questions, I have learned through creative recovery that it is possible to understand why you may have made the choices you made, whether you see your life as a masterpiece or not. Most importantly, with effort, we can begin listening for something in the music of our lives that we may be missing, a hidden gem or resolution that's waiting to resonate.

Hearing your life is a deep dive into the self—listening for the themes, details, and truths that are there. It can feel like looking at your pores up close in the mirror. But what I didn't realize back in school, what I've learned working with creatives, is that doing the inner work of *that* hearing is the best way to find a sustainable, joyful, resonant creative life. It opens us up to ourselves, our art, and others. We learn to make decisions, even very difficult ones, from a place of truth and integrity. We become a witness to all that happens to us instead of the critical judge who heaps shame upon our heads. We learn that we have innate value and worthiness regardless of how we perform.

TOOLS FOR HEARING

Daily self-reflection is the main tool we use for hearing our life in creative recovery. This is the power of Julia Cameron's "Morning Pages," described in the étude, three longhand stream-of-conscious journaling exercises that are completed first thing upon waking. These practices may feel like busy work, but I have seen them open artists to a deep inner creative thriving and spiritual resonance. At the end of the chapter, you'll find a menu of self-reflective practices. These simple tools for hearing can help you foster a restorative self-reflection experience that encourages you to show up again and again to hear all your life is saying to you. To better hear what our lives have to say, here are some principles to keep in mind:

1. **Ask the right questions.**

Panetti always had us ask very specific questions of a score. Highlighters (ink!) were her tool of choice. We'd scour the sheet music with bright pinks, yellows, and blues, looking for specifics. We'd chart and mark them, watch for their evolution, and listen for throughlines. Hearing your life means asking the right questions of it. Letting them be the primary tool with which you uncover your own patterns and themes. Throughout this book, the self-coaching questions are merely a starting point. Learning to ask the right question at the right time is crucial to creative recovery.

2. **Live your life live.**

Like great classical music, your life was meant to be experienced in real time. Panetti knew that the magic of music was watching the performer and the composer "interact" as the music unfolded live.

Are you showing up to listen to what your life is saying to you today, this very minute? We miss hearing today when we live in the past or the future. Your self-reflection practice will give you a clear view of where your thoughts tend to go; cultivating mindfulness and presence takes effort, but if we train our ears to listen for it, there is something for us to hear in this very moment.

3. **Zoom in, zoom out.**

Studying a great masterpiece involves not missing the macro for the micro. Sometimes the inconsequential gestures can be the crux of the masterpiece. It can be easy to get lost in the minutiae of our daily lives, letting the frustrations and disappointments make us lose our perspective of the whole picture. You may wonder how whining about how tired you are in your journal is going to help you feel more creative. Self-reflection helps us empty the trash of our minds. We release it and move on or let it reveal what it is we really want.

The goal is not to get lost in complaining or ruminating. Hearing is a safe posture for taking things apart and noticing how each section works with the whole.

WHAT WAS THERE ALL ALONG

Mia's musical car rides are a perfect example. We need only sing along to all that our lives are saying. Sometimes the best way to hear is to sing the music for yourself.

Sometimes the best way to hear is to sing the music for yourself.

From our work in the group, Mia considered joining a choir, and after her divorce was final, she actually tried one. But when she showed up to that first rehearsal, she realized she didn't want to share her voice. For now, her singing was just for her. It was her time to exhale, to sing at the top of her lungs, and to hear to all the things she wasn't saying.

Bach's cello suites were written between 1717 and 1723, and, like many of Bach's works, these pieces remained largely ignored until the next century. The cello suites, some of the most popular and recognizable classical music today, were finally published in 1825, but were viewed as exercises for students. A young Pablo Casals, a Catalan cellist prodigy, discovered an old edition in a music store in 1889, and it was Casals who first heard their genius.

Like a Bach cello suite, you are something to be studied, valued, uncovered, and revealed to yourself and the world. Great works of art are lovely to enjoy for leisure without having to dive deep into their technicalities and meaning, but when you "hear" them like Panetti taught us, you see much more than their loveliness. You see the intricacies of how they contain complex dissonance and thematic cycles.

In Bach and the rest of the Western classical canon, themes always return. Maybe these musical greats liked the symmetry, or maybe we need to hear things multiple times before we get the message. Our lives are episodes of great expression, detours, and seemingly inexplicable left turns. Yet, we can see the process differently when we know where we are headed. Listening to your life and hearing it can feel fun, terrible, harrowing, and joyful; it can feel like coming home, like reading a book you've read a million times but never totally understood. It can make you feel angry about the time you've lost or relieved that in spite of resting on your shelf for all those years, the album still plays.

Know this: Your life still sings, whether you hear it or not. And maybe you'll have a moment like I did in the back of that musty auditorium, on the second or third time through, where you hear it, hidden in the inner voices, the simplest theme returning again, again.

What are the themes resonating in your life? *You are loved. That is enough. This is your purpose. This is who you are.*

Self-reflection allows us to hear what was there all along, hidden in plain sight, waiting to be returned to us.

SELF-COACHING QUESTIONS

1. Look back at the answers from the étude in chapter 1. What truths are you hearing your life speak through your history?

2. What are the themes of your life? How do your responses to circumstances reveal what matters to you?

3. What gives you energy? What parts of your life make you come alive?

4. Write a list of your wildest dreams. What do you want?

5. Who in your life allows you to show up as your true self, and who are the "crazy makers" who usurp your energy and time?

ÉTUDE: LISTEN TO YOUR LIFE

The greatest way to hear your life speak is to listen to your own thoughts. Julia Cameron's Morning Pages have brought clarity and breakthrough to many of us, but they are not the only way to achieve self-reflection, to hear your own inner chatter. Below are some exercises I have collected to help you do this. Try them and see which one works best for you.

1. Morning Pages: Julia Cameron instructs readers to write "three pages of stream-of-consciousness writing each day first thing upon waking." Don't let the name fool you; these pages are powerful at any time of day.

2. Homework for life: Storyteller Matthew Dicks recommends writing one sentence before bed about something memorable from your day to collect potential story ideas. Answer this question: What was story-worthy in your life today?

3. Record yourself speaking: Use a voice memo or walkie-talkie app and complete the sentence, "Today I feel . . ." or "Today I want it known that . . ." Send the message to yourself.

4. Sit down and make two lists: "What Is Wrong" and "What Is Right." When you feel anxious, it can be useful

to list all the things on your mind. Categorizing them as right and wrong might seem simplistic but resist the temptation to analyze them or to start problem-solving. Let these lists show you all you carry, good and bad.

Just like you are not supposed to share or even reread your Morning Pages, these exercises aim to help your inner voices let off steam, not uncover creative gems. Although you will find that, especially with the daily repetition of self-reflection, you may eventually hear truths leading you to take action, uncovering dreams or goals after you've mentioned them twelve days in a row. Resist the temptation to edit yourself as you let the reflection come out. Think of it like emptying the trash of your brain or rinsing the espresso machine before you make the coffee.

One more tip: These exercises are recommended for you to do daily and dovetail nicely with the creative devotion routine we set forth in chapter 3. Whichever self-reflection exercise you choose, the spirit behind the task is more important than the task itself: hear your life speak and meet whatever you hear with curiosity instead of judgment.

CODA ⊕

Fractals are mathematical sets, first named by mathematician Benoit Mandelbrot in 1975, that display similarly at whatever scale—that is, they look the same no matter how big or small. Fractals are one way we describe the patterned disorder found in nature, and they are everywhere in the natural world. Take trees, for example; there is a pattern of the trunk putting down roots on one end and limbs on the other, with a smaller repetition found on the branch and leaf. Once you notice fractals, you realize that nature constantly repeats patterns at different scales. Trees and plants look like they grow wildly, but it's a predictable wildness, patterned chaos. I love that mother nature is design savvy, swirling a certain abundant, uncontainable, interconnected chaos of beauty.

What is your life saying to you through patterned chaos? What if your life was a fractal, and whatever you create, whatever you're becoming, what if it's not random or siloed but part of a larger pattern of swirling mayhem that is your life? You may think that looking internally and seeking to be a joyful artist or happy person is self-serving or self-indulgent, that getting creatively unblocked helps no one but yourself. But nature tells us otherwise, doesn't it?

> *What if your life was a fractal, and whatever you create, whatever you're becoming, what if it's not random or siloed but part of a larger pattern of swirling mayhem that is your life?*

Every part is connected to the whole, and when we artists get healthy and prioritize finding our way into our own joyful living, it becomes a fractal, repeating at whatever scale.

You listen to your life and create art that helps people listen to theirs, and they create more, and suddenly joy spreads like seeds in the wind, like rivers branching from a source. Looking at all the world's problems, you may be tempted to think that you and your creative work are obsolete, but nature works in fractals, and you're part of nature. Hearing your life speak does more than change your art; it can change the world.

You and your seemingly unpatterned life are beautiful like romesco broccoli. There is a purpose to it, a pattern that may not always be visible but, when you look closer, you see it connects you to the world around you, unique and infinitely repeated.

Martha Beck, who first taught me about fractals in her book *The Way of Integrity*, says, "As a twig is to a branch is to a tree trunk, so is one human's integrity to a couple's, a family's, a nation's. This is how individuals and small groups may end up influencing huge numbers of people." Here's to listening deeply to what all our lives are saying to us in joy, letting the patterned chaos lead us to our own healing and to the healing of the world.

Five True Things (the last one is yours to add):

1. Daydreaming is productive for the artist.

2. "The present is the only time in which any duty may be done or grace received" (C. S. Lewis).

3. "No feeling is final" (Rainer Maria Rilke).

4. Daily self-reflection is integral to creative recovery.

5. FRACTALS!

FIVE

Ode to Dreaming

Casting Vision, Crafting Goals, and Taking Action

Prelude in C Major, BWV 846, by J. S. Bach

Whatever you think you can do or believe you can do, begin it. Action has magic, grace and power in it.

—Attributed to Johann Wolfgang von Goethe

KARL

He was a shell of himself after he lost his wife. The week he had retired from teaching studio art and sculpture at a small liberal arts college, she'd gotten the stage-four news. When she died six months later, amidst the wreckage of his grief, Karl saw our ad online and joined the creative recovery group. One day, he told the class that his life seemed like a large and lonely abyss spread out before him. He had no idea what to do with his days now that no one was left to care for or mentor.

Karl was getting antsy, even agitated, a few weeks into the course. I wasn't surprised at all when he stopped coming. But I *was* surprised when I received this email from him a few months later:

Dear Merideth, Greetings from Bismarck, North Dakota!

I'm writing now to thank you.

Our creativity group made me remember something I'd dreamt of doing since I was a kid, so I thought it best to go do that. I'm so sorry for leaving without notice.

He explained how he had been obsessed with dinosaurs as a boy. When he learned that there was a program that paired museums and paleontologists with anyone from the public interested in joining a real dig, he applied for the program immediately. When his wife's health turned, he had forgotten all about the idea.

With almost unbelievable synchronicity, after her death, three weeks into our creative recovery group, Karl got a call saying there was an unexpected opening on the next dig. So off he went to follow his dream.

Karl's email continued:

In the end, I did reach my goal of finding at least something—a tooth fragment with a so-far-unknown origin. The best part though, was the experience of the dig itself. Who knew that hours and hours of nothing could be so engaging? Brushing and looking and tapping and listening, brushing, and looking and tapping and listening, over and over again, and then hours or days later: BOOM! Hope shines through in the form of a dark and dirty something in the earth.

THE TASMANIAN DEVIL IN A ONESIE

While Karl was knee-deep in the old, I was raising the new. My two-and-a-half-year-old daughter, Eva, has these occasional moments before bedtime where she completely loses it. She tells me she wants everything for dinner and then eats nothing. She becomes obsessed with the idea of playing with Play-Doh, and then when we do, she cries that we aren't playing fairies. In search of the fairies, she gets an insane burst of energy, runs laps around the kitchen island for a while, trips over said fairies, bumps her head, says she wants water, and says, "NO NO NO! Not the blue cup . . . the purple cup!" and on and on and on. It took us a while, but my husband and I finally realized our child had not been replaced by a moody Tasmanian devil. She was just tired.

Since we welcomed this little human, my main job as a mother has surprised me. I am, first and foremost, a translator. I am the one to decode what in the world this screaming bundle of chaos really wants or needs. It starts with the CIA-level crash course in cry interpretation. And just when you think it would be easier when they gain language skills, it turns out toddlers still can't tell you what they need in a given moment because they don't know what they need in any given moment.

One evening, at the end of a long day of parenting (more specifically, parenting when I really needed to write), I found myself wrangling my screaming toddler into the bathtub like a kitten with claws out. I knelt down in her bathroom, the front of my jeans soaking wet. I somehow managed to get the flailing noodle from the bath to the bed, where, by God's grace, I finished the rest of the bedtime routine.

Then the most incredible thing happened. We sat in the darkness rocking, and suddenly and unceremoniously, Eva surrendered.

There was just enough light for me to see her face, her eyes were blinking more slowly. Her limbs, which moments before were cocked like branches ready to slap me in the face, relaxed and released. For a while, she stared up at the ceiling, but then her eyes rested squarely on mine. There we are, together in this moment of complete stillness. She hadn't let me hold her like this since infancy. She doesn't move her eyes away, I don't dare move mine, and then in the silence, I smiled. She smiled back. I laughed, and she laughed. Neither of us moved our gaze for at least a whole minute. This is a small miracle.

As I locked eyes with this thirty-pound wild animal, I felt my limbs release too. I let go of the long day of dress-up and Play-Doh and all the thrown food that was waiting for me on the kitchen walls. I released stress and anxiety around my writing deadline, and I just looked at Eva. She looked at me.

We both get exactly what we don't know we need: sixty seconds of lucid tenderness and the pure joy of being seen.

THE ARTIST'S TANTRUM

It's easy to judge a toddler in those moments of intense overtiredness. Lord knows I judge her. But I think I'm judgmental because when I see this lack of self-awareness and self-control (which, for a toddler, is perfectly normal), it reminds me of myself.

I see mini-tantrums in my creative recovery class and coaching clients as well. We, adults, don't know what we need from moment to moment either, or we know and aren't ready to admit it. Our tantrums look like: resistance, shutting down, overreacting, a feigned lack of interest. Or, for artists, in the words of Julia Cameron, the sudden Creative U-turn. We are presented with a creative opportunity, and we promptly about-face. We create an emotional diversion to hide all the things we are burying, from our basic needs to our deepest desires and dreams. Instead of imperative and necessary, we call our needs, desires, and dreams impractical, wasteful, and stupid. We even deny ourselves what we need out of fear or self-hatred. We self-sabotage. We chase after the wrong things out of duty or obligation, we put others before ourselves until there is nothing left of us (which seems virtuous but is very much not), we run ourselves ragged checking all the boxes, so busy, yet so bored, so full, yet so hungry.

Emily McDowell said, "'Finding yourself' is not really how it works. You aren't a ten-dollar bill in last winter's coat pocket. You are also not lost. Your true self is right there, buried under cultural conditioning, other people's opinions, and inaccurate conclusions you drew as a kid that became your beliefs about who you are. 'Finding yourself' is actually returning to yourself. An unlearning, an excavation, a remembering who you were before the world got its hands on you." What we truly want is buried someplace deep within us, safely out of sight.

The world hasn't gotten its hands too much on Eva yet, so her gaze reminded me that night. When she trusted me to give her what she needed and agreed that she was tired—or I had finally worn her down—I realized, as I held her calm body, that she and I are not so different. Staring into her eyes was the beginning of an excavation, she was returning myself to me.

I have found the process of finding myself, my needs, and my deepest desires much more challenging than Eva. I had finally taken this big leap, devoting time to writing, a deeply buried dream I thought I had to sacrifice on the altar of being a professional oboist. And yet, with all the writing I had been doing during the cracks of motherhood, every week, I still felt so behind.

I was judging every word I wrote and a joylessness was creeping in again. Instead of letting the enormous surge of energy that comes with taking action carry me through the tough days, my mind was running laps around the kitchen island of my fear.

I hadn't realized that when we uncover a buried dream, we often stand on the site of some kind of wreckage. Like Karl, in the dinosaur field, you might not even be sure of what you're standing there looking at. But please know, with every buried dream we unearth comes stirred-up clouds of sadness and grief, wasted time, the past wounds. The repercussions of our delay blindside us—*It's too late. What's the point? Who do I think I am?*—these can cause tantrums, but without courage, they can also stop us from digging altogether.

> *I hadn't realized that when we uncover a buried dream, we often stand on the site of some kind of wreckage.*

This is where the world had its way with me: underneath my tantrum about becoming a writer was a belief—a fear—that people only get one great dream in their lives. This little girl from small-town South Carolina had gotten to perform all over the world on the oboe; I had achieved a certain level of success at such a niche thing. Not only that, I'd married a man I loved and had a precious daughter. But God was done giving me dreams.

As I held Eva's gaze, I heard her calling me out of my tantrum with her child-like hope, showing me what I really needed; it was as if she was saying: "Write this."

So, I decided in that moment to be the parent to both Eva and to myself. Because I know that regardless of what Eva says she wants, when it is 7:00 p.m., it's time to sleep. And the same is true for me; when it is 5:00 a.m., I know, regardless of how much I want to sleep or how much resistance I feel, it is time to write.

I get up and make some coffee, and I type type type because that's what writers do.

DIGGING FOR DREAMS

You get as many dreams as you want in this life, of course you do. The field is ripe for the digging. So go ahead and admit it to yourself. Buy the paints, write the email, set your alarm, sign up for the class, dust off your dreams a little more each day, even when you don't feel like it.

And when you have a tantrum, remember Eva. Remember how, when she gets like that, those of us who love her rush in and lead her, kicking and screaming, to the crib where she will rest and wake up her cheerful self. We work hard to love and know her well enough to anticipate her needs, so she doesn't get overtired. Maybe your inner artist-child needs a translator, and needs a parent, too.

All the dreams you have had since you were Eva's size are buried within you. Regardless of how deep you've buried them, they're still down there, fossilized in fear. A tantrum is usually just your inner artist trying to tell you something. It is simply a matter of slowing down long enough to catch those dreams' gaze, to have the courage to look them right in the eye. When you see through the tantrums of scarcity and fear, you'll find yourself being returned to you. And when that happens, you can't help but smile at the joy and tenderness of hope you find there in the dirt.

An artist friend told me that this method, subtractive sculpting, where the artist uses a hammer and chisel, and basically gets one chance to free the angel in the marble, is like working through the soul of the stone. He's in good company: the great Italian Renaissance sculptor Michelangelo is often quoted, "Every block of stone has a statue inside it and it is the task of the sculptor to discover it. I saw the angel in the marble and I carved until I set him free."

This art form also sounds very stressful. Yet there is something beautiful about this image that moves me: the only thing separating big rocks from great art is a matter of editing. Maybe it isn't about creating something out of nothing but stripping away stone until you reach the skin of an angel.

Yet there is something beautiful about this image that moves me: the only thing separating big rocks from great art is a matter of editing.

SELF-COACHING QUESTIONS

1. How do you most want your life to be different in this season?

2. What stories are you telling yourself about any of the wildest dreams you listed in chapter 4?

3. What are your dreams buried under? What do you use for blocks?

4. Have you had a tantrum lately? What was it about? What did it feel like?

5. Who in your life do you share your creative frustrations with?

ÉTUDE: A WELL-CRAFTED GOAL

Dreams become reality when we take action toward our goals. And yet goals can be creative blocks in and of themselves. Coaching clients come to me ready to take steps toward their dreams but immediately feel stuck by the immense weight of what lies ahead.

George Doran put forth the S.M.A.R.T. goals paradigm in 1981 to help those in corporate America set goals that were specific, measurable, achievable, relevant, and time-bound. These criteria can be great for task-driven goals. However, over the years, I have found that creative coaching clients have struggled with making their artistic practice and creative goals fit into this system for several reasons. The main one is that many times we can dream about creative achievements (winning the Grammy, getting a big job, traditionally publishing a novel), but anyone who has tried to achieve these things knows that no matter how specific or measurable or relevant the goal is, so much of the outcome is completely out of our control. It is easy to feel like a failure when the goals you make as a creative are not met.

What if there was a way to set goals that celebrates all that is beautiful about the creative process? A framework that reminds us that the most important thing about our goals is the resilient, healthy, joyful person we are becoming in achieving them. Then, regardless of the outcome, we become the kind of person who wins a Grammy, even if we do not see that specific accolade allotted to us in our lifetime. A different framework could allow us to find joy in our pursuit of success and, more importantly, to define success for ourselves.

In chapter 4, you wrote down your wildest dreams. You learned that daydreaming and self-reflection are productive for the creator. Instead of S.M.A.R.T. goals, we will use a new paradigm, C.R.A.F.T., to distill the goals from our dreams. It's important to distinguish between the two, goals and dreams, because we must leave space in the creative process to be led, to discover and, most importantly, to resist the temptation that so many of us have to equate our achievements with our value as a person.

In this framework, you will:

Create process, not product

Recruit the help you need

Align work with your values

Frame the work with constraints that enable

Twist and turn, but keep stepping forward

1. Take a dream from the coaching questions in chapter 4.

2. Read each of the prompts below and translate the dream into goals or actions to take within the C.R.A.F.T. parameters. I've written a real-life example for you from my life and one from an imaginary guitarist coaching client.

Dream—Traditionally publish a nonfiction book about well-being for artists.

Dream—Win a Grammy by age fifty.

Create process, not product: What goals/actions allow me to enjoy the process while making the dream product? Any artist knows that you learn so much by doing. Sustainable and joyful goals are driven not by the end product but by what is right in front of you each day. That's all you can control anyway. A well-C.R.A.F.T.ed goal's first step is cultivating a sustainable, daily creative practice that is more about devotion than discipline.

Goal: Write every morning.

Goal: Practice scale patterns every night before bed.

Recruit the help you need: You aren't expected to know everything. Finding the right partners and resources that will help you move toward your goal without over-whelming or discouraging you is key. We will discuss the process of naming whose feedback you absorb in chapter 7, but as it pertains to your goals, the recruitment phase reminds you that asking for help is a normal and healthy part of making progress.

Goal: Take a nonfiction book proposal writing course. Find a writing coach.

Goal: Join an online songwriting critique group.

Align the work with your values: When you craft goals that align with what matters most to you, with a desired future view of yourself, then you can hold the award, accolade, or achievement loosely because (while it would be nice to publish the book or win the Grammy) in the end there are many things outside of our control in creative endeavors. Focusing on becoming the kind of person you want to be, instead of winning an arbitrary achievement, allows you to shoot for the moon and land among the stars.

Goal: Create coaching resources that help artists thrive (motivated by my deeply held belief that all people are capable and whole).

Goal: Take some lessons from a Latin jazz specialist (motivated by the deeply held belief that music from all cultures has something to teach me).

Frame the work with constraints that enable you: C.R.A.F.T. goals live within time constraints, but not in the same way as S.M.A.R.T. goals. Like a frame around a painting, enabling constraints provides focus and clarity without blocking the artistic process. Examples of enabling constraints include a schedule that prioritizes your most creative hours, limiting your audience, or using one artistic medium and not another. Nikki's strict vocal regime (chapter 2) is a frame she uses to feel her best. C.R.A.F.T. goals have boundaries that move projects along when they need to but are flexible enough not to burn out or overwhelm the artist. A well-placed deadline is the most powerful enabling constraint there is.

Goal: Publish something small every Friday online.

Goal: Take on a few more private students so I can phase out of wedding gigs to have more time to write music on the weekends.

Twist and turn, but keep stepping forward: Artists don't always go from A to B. Sometimes it looks more like: A to Q, B to S to Z to A, and back. Learning fast music requires you to slow it down, which can sound like the opposite of progress. Small steps in an often nonlinear direction can add up to incredible, sustainable progress, especially when you combine the zigzag stepping with the frames that focus. A clear path from start to finish makes us miss the joy of experimentation and learning through play. C.R.A.F.T. goals consider and make space for us to enjoy the twists and turns, encouraging the creator to take the next small step in a particular direction (to go after the magic, grace, and power that Goethe spoke of) even when they cannot see what is around the bend.

Goal: Send queries to literary agents in rounds so I can implement the feedback I receive.

Goal: Pick songs for the album by playing them one by one with curiosity instead of judgment.

Your turn:

Dream (choose one from chapter 4 or write a new one):

List of things you are already doing toward this dream:

Now, let's C.R.A.F.T. your goals.

Create a process, not a product.

- What actions allow me to enjoy my process while making my dream product?
- What does my creative routine look like? How is it serving me?
- You know a goal is helping create a process when it feels: sustainable, open, consistent, and repeatable.

GOAL:

Recruit the help you need.

- What information do I need to move forward with this dream? Who or what can help answer my questions, overcome obstacles, and hold me accountable?
- If you aren't sure what help you need, look at the tasks or mindsets keeping you most stuck. Make them as small as possible. What information do you need to move forward now? As Emily P. Freeman's book encourages us, ask: "What's the next right thing to do in love?"

- You know when a goal is helping you recruit when it feels: resourced, supported, unstuck, and motivated.

GOAL:

Align the goal with who you want to become.

- What actions help me become the kind of person who achieves this dream? What deeply held beliefs of mine inform my creative offerings?

- You know when a goal is aligned when it feels: resonant, inspiring, aspirational, and hopeful.

GOAL:

Frame the work with constraints that enable you.

- Where in your goal can you name the barriers or points of order that will enable you to move forward? (You've likely already used frames when you named your creative process. Try to pin down more.)

- You know when a goal uses frames when it feels: contained, boundaried, achievable, and nonoverwhelming.

GOAL:

Twist and turn, but keep stepping forward.

- What twists and turns have you encountered so far in pursuing this dream? How can you support yourself in that process?

- What is the next small step forward in the nonlinear dance that is creative success?

- You know when a goal makes space for the twists and turns when it feels: fun, playful, experimental, curious, and adaptive.

GOAL:

CODA ⊕

When I see Michelangelo's work, all his talent and technique—the towering David, which is nearly three times life-size, the folds of Mary's cloaks in the Pietá—I experience what critics of the day called *terribilitá* or intense awe. But what we forget is the terrible loss that led to Michelangelo becoming a sculptor in the first place. His mother was sick most of his early life and died when he was six. He was sent to live with a nanny whose husband was a stonecutter. Legend has it that little Michelangelo grew up playing with stone-cutting tools at his nanny's home; the rest is history. There it was again, the stripping away; this great loss in his life revealed the sculptor within him.

What in your life is being chiseled away? What might this loss be revealing in you? Maybe you, like me, don't like it when people say, "Everything happens for a reason," when there's pain or grief. I prefer this image of Michelangelo chiseling away, harnessing the artist's power to see things working together for good. Among all the dust and marble scraps on the sculptor's floor, he must have believed there was meaning buried there. Maybe all we need is tools, time, and vision to turn the dreams buried within us into concrete action. May we all have the strength to see them, patience for the carving, and the courage to set them free.

Five True Things (don't forget to add yours):

1. Creative goals aren't necessarily S.M.A.R.T.—small, measurable, achievable, relevant, or time-bound—this doesn't mean they are invalid or crazy.

2. Asking the right questions matters more than the answers you receive to the wrong ones.

3. Saying no to one thing means saying yes to others.

4. Sometimes, the next right thing is the dishes.

5. *Gathering support is part of the process.*

PART TWO

Development
Artist in the World

də'veləpmənt/

1. The process of developing or being developed.

2. The middle section of sonata form, characterized by its tonal instability, thematic episodes, and exploration of formal organization.

You need to claim the events of your life to make yourself yours.

—Florida Scott-Maxwell, *The Measure of My Days*

Introduction to Part II
Thematic Transformation

Joy is taking the theme's hand and letting it lift you off your feet, watching its development as you encounter the world.

You know the theme so well now that you could dictate it from memory. It is your *Leitmotif* (the theme that plays when a specific character walks on stage in an opera). It comes from the verb "to lead." Will you rest in the music's arms, move in sync with it, let it lead you like a trusted partner?

We've passed the secondary theme, the closing material of the exposition. It seems we are coming to a close, but something sounds different. The original tone and tenor of the melody have shifted slightly. There's been a modulation of color. We have not ended where we began. There's a double bar, which signifies a type of ending, but a completely new section starts at the turn of the page.

Where did the theme go? It's appearing in part without the whole. The first few notes are in the flutes, the next three are played loudly with force in the trumpets. The orchestra has taken the melody and broken it apart. Something that felt so complete and resonant has some instability to it now, exciting, but unsettling too. The theme's second half is inverted, slowed way down in the violas. It's hard to hear because it's hidden in the lush orchestration, but it's there. Someone took your puzzle pieces, put them in a bag, and shook them up; now they are being pulled out individually. This episodic journey sounds cacophonous, but it's still beautiful in its own way. Each section of the orchestra intends to leave no stone unturned in it. What will it become?

In part II, we will explore how to take our creative work to the world while staying joyful in the face of all that development. We will explore how to find your people as you "claim the events of your life" and seek to "make yourself yours," as Florida Scott-Maxwell urges. We will discuss how to manage reception and rejection, make decisions, and finally, how to stop comparing yourself to others.

SIX

Ode to Belonging

Why Being You Is Better Than Being Normal

"Much More," from *The Fantasticks*,
by Tom Jones, featuring Harvey Schmidt and Rita Gardner

Anybody who has survived his childhood has enough
information about life to last him the rest of his days.
　　　　　　—Flannery O'Connor, *Mystery and Manners*

NAOMI

She travels with a gallon-size Ziploc because you
never know what you might find. Some people in
her life find her obsession with discarded objects (i.e.,
trash) quite weird. It is not uncommon to find her
coming back from a walk with a wet and dirty mitten,
a uniquely colored glass bottle found on the riverbank,
or an interestingly shaped stick. She sees these things
underfoot that others would miss and takes them home
to add to her collection. To her, the world is full of trea-
sures, if you are willing to look down. She makes intricate and precious things out of her findings—sculptures
and jewelry, mostly. Her largest project to date was a
small meditation cell in her backyard: a round hut, the
walls speckled with sea glass and other found objects,

held in place with mud she'd mixed into homemade cement and stacked sticks.

Once, her therapist had pointed out to her (the way therapists do) that maybe she loved lost objects so much because she identified with them. Naomi herself had left home at sixteen and over the last three decades she'd worked to build the kind of life her drug-addicted mother and absent father could never give her. As we stood inside the flimsy structure she'd built on the edge of her property, made with lost things found, I realized then what a holy place it was. I grabbed her hand and told her so.

In the hands of the artist, the broken and lost belong.

MY CHILDHOOD SECRET

From the hilltop by the fence at the stadium named after my grandfather, you could watch the hot South Carolina sun sink into the ground, smells of childhood floating through the heavy air: cut grass and fried food, mainly. The name on the sign (my grandfather was the coach when they built it), the location of my own father's chairs (he would go early each Friday morning to stake his claim), my sister as a cheerleader, my brothers being primed for quarterback status since the womb, this was all proof—my family was a *sports family.*

But as I sat at the top of the hill at that stadium, heiress to the throne, I had a secret (delicious, boiled peanuts notwithstanding): I did not like sports.

I was bored a millisecond after kickoff at the football games. How barbaric! Baseball was mind-numbingly slow; basketball always smelled like sweat. And then there was the fear of flying objects hitting me in the face. Not liking sports in my family made me the Baldwin brother who wouldn't act. As I barreled closer and closer to adolescence, I had that sinking feeling: something was wrong with me. I didn't like what everyone else liked.

My parents didn't bat an eyelash when I repeatedly blared Barbara Streisand in my bedroom. They let me do whatever extracurricular activities I wanted: band, drama club, and special art. (I wanted to ride horses—a sport, by the way—but there were no stables where kids could ride in our town.) Even when they approved of my extracurriculars, choosing not to tow the family line as a sports person felt illicit. I was eleven or twelve when I started spending as much time as possible at the Opera House.

DON'T LET ME BE NORMAL

The old brick building had its own smell—musty but woody and clean. Beneath all the red carpet, the hardwood whined predictably with this sense of reassurance; the whole place seemed alive with music and memory. I look back on it and realize the fact that such a gem of a community theater existed in my small southern town was a miracle. It might as well have been Broadway.

My parents mercifully let me volunteer as an usher, even on Friday nights during football season. Ushering meant I could see the shows weekend after weekend for free. Even at that age, I knew: the passion I didn't feel at the stadium, I felt for a creaky-floored theater on the end of the town square. This was where I belonged.

One fall at the opera house, they did a musical called *The Fantasticks* by Tom Jones. I ushered the entire run. Night after night, I'd sit in the back of the theater with the other ushers and watch the actors create a world that was mine. Luisa, one character in that show, knows she's different and longs to see the world. Her one line always made the audience chuckle: "Please, God, please! Don't let me be normal!"

When this moment happened in the show each night, I would mouth the words with her like my own prayer: *Please, God, please don't let me be normal.* It felt like being seen, being released from an imaginary sentence; it gave me hope.

But right on the heels of those feelings of exhilaration came a very adult kind of sadness. I started to wonder what the reality of not being "normal" might mean. If I decided that I wasn't staying in South Carolina, to be bold about my decision to be at the Opera House instead of the stadium, what would become of me? And would leading that life, instead of the one I thought everyone expected of me, mean being alone?

FINDING MY PEOPLE

Once I started acting in plays myself, when I got to be backstage around the other older actors, I used to watch them closely for clues. I was in awe of their wildness and freedom, unapologetic boldness, and complete disregard for what other people thought of them. I had no idea there were people like that in the world. These were my people.

Mo, the Artful Dodger, had been married twice by age thirty and always wore shirts where you could see her bra. James, Daddy Warbucks, always smelled like his special cigarettes and once played a practical joke on Ms. Hanigan, too raunchy for the pages of this text. Through the dressing room walls, I heard cackling and four-letter words. And on stage, their voices held up the proscenium arch. The hall might as well have been named after them. They were magic.

After the show, they would leave through the stage door into the night. I imagined them going to some apartment where the fridge was empty. I sensed that, as far as my community was concerned, being an artist came with a certain kind of separateness, and I realized the loneliness followed me home to my childhood bedroom like smoke on my clothes. Like many artsy kids, I wore it like a badge of honor. Being with others who felt different helped me no longer feel like a liability. The Opera House gave me the confidence to go out into the world and find more of my people, to believe they were out there.

And that's what I did when I left home for good for arts boarding school for my final years of high school, then on to music conservatory, and life as a professional musician. While choosing the theater instead of the stadium at age twelve meant, in some ways, leaving my family, I knew this was my path, and I have never looked back.

WE MAKE WORLDS

Artists know something special about belonging; I've coached enough artists and played enough gigs with strangers (friends by the downbeat) to see it firsthand. Maybe because so many of us felt like misfits growing up, or maybe the act of creating itself is a kind of community maker—we make worlds in our work where we feel safe and invite others to join us there.

Maybe because so many of us felt like misfits growing up, or maybe the act of creating itself is a kind of community maker—we make worlds in our work where we feel safe and invite others to join us there.

And yet, claiming the title "artist" as an adult has taught me that belonging means not only something we make, but simply stepping into someone we already are. Watching for the moments when your life whispers (or even screams), *Pay attention! This is for you.* We so often feel like we must create our identity, perhaps because we have wondered if we fit.

Who you are, where you belong, it is already in you; it is just a matter of being awake, being open to seeing it when it comes into the light from backstage, and being brave enough to accept the community that is waiting for you there. For me, the opera house was my first glimpse at real belonging. Where was it for you? The band room, the studio, the library? Take it from a theater nerd; do not wear the costume of another. The first step in belonging is to ask yourself what makes you come alive and follow it with all your heart, despite what kind of family you're born into or what everyone expects you to be.

As an artist, you may feel separate or different or lonely, but I believe we know something special about belonging because creating makes us open to seeing the world as it could be instead of how it is. Like Naomi and her found objects, we deem things others may discard as valuable because we tend to see ourselves in them. We can look at the whole world, even each other, with our artist-eye—with curiosity and wonder and acceptance, not judgment. We can offer friendship and community to others, not expecting them to change or complete us, but to inspire us, to make us think, to make us laugh, and to do all the things any great work of art can do.

I agree with Flannery O'Connor—surviving childhood gives a wealth of information about life, and I was one of the lucky ones. Even though I am the only one in my family who left our small town, even though I'm the only one who followed a different path, or as my mother says, "marched to the beat of my own oboe," my family has shown me support and love—they helped me through those turbulent years of adolescence, they showed me that the stadium vs. opera house was not an either/or, that I can belong in our family even though I am different. They gave me lots of opportunities to show up as myself. I felt loved, even when we weren't together on Friday nights.

That may not be your experience. Not every kid gets that kind of acceptance, and I don't take it lightly. Maybe you are still searching for that sense of belonging, that community where you found your people. Maybe you're like Naomi, and you look back at all the trauma you have withstood and wonder how you could ever belong again. Maybe that loneliness you have always sensed in being different, maybe it doesn't so much follow you as it does completely envelop you. Maybe you are asking yourself the same questions I asked in the dark theater in my hometown: Is it possible as an artist to cultivate stable relationships that encourage, fortify, and offer us the acceptance we long for? Am I alone?

We artists have this invaluable resource around us: each other. We can share our experiences, struggles, triumphs, and joys in the dressing room and in whatever world we make together. We need not only turn them into great art but relish in the little community of realness that can make the theater people, the band people, the arts people, and yes, the sports people— all those who long to be themselves—know they are accepted and loved, just as they are. Show up as yourself, use your artist's eye to love others well,

> *We artists have this invaluable resource around us: each other.*

and—regardless of how broken or discarded you may feel when relationships end or your community fails you—know that lonely, broken things can be valued, cherished, and made beautiful again by the artist.

SELF-COACHING QUESTIONS

1. When do you feel safe to be yourself?

2. Write a short list completing the prompt: "In this family, we . . ." What kinds of things did your childhood family believe? What unspoken or spoken rules did you live by growing up?

3. As you create your own life (and in some cases seek out another iteration of family), what are the rules you choose to live by now?

4. What communities belong to you? Whose voices have been historically silenced? How are you working to help others sense their belovedness and experience true belonging?

5. Who in your life reminds you of your freedom to belong?

ÉTUDE: SELF-PORTRAIT

In chapter 1, you compared your childhood self to your adult self. In this étude, we will live in the present, looking more closely at ourselves as we are today. Research has shown that when we connect with what we like about ourselves, what matters most to us, and other positive emotions, we feel more motivation, inspiration, and other adaptive behaviors that lead to growth and change. Scientists like Anita Howard of Case Western Reserve University call this Intentional Change Theory, using Positive Emotional Attractors (PEA) and Emotional Intelligence. The clearer the picture we get of ourselves, the more we can make decisions from a place of strength, even when taking action is hard. The more self-actualized we become, the more joyful we become, because we live in congruence with our own inner integrity. We become more resilient, learning to cope better with life's stressors. We experience a sense of belonging when we first know and accept who we are. Or as Brené Brown reminds us, "Belonging is belonging to yourself first."

There are numerous ways coaches and researchers get people to connect with PEA, like visualizations, coaching questions, and choosing from long lists of value words. In this exercise, I will prompt you to answer with what comes to mind first. Answer in bulleted lists or however the information comes; consider who you are today, at this moment. What you write does not have to be true for all time and eternity. (These questions make for a fun date or time with friends if you are someone who likes to externally process or finds themselves distracted when doing things like this on their own.)

With the answers, the next step is to look deeper into their meaning. Graydin's Start with Heart model begins with helping the coachee connect to their values as a key component of well-being and fulfillment in each coaching session. As you go through these lists, choose a few words that encapsulate what is at the *heart* of your answer. Beside each one, see if you can narrow it down to one or two words or a simple phrase and write it in the heart column.

List a few of your favorites, and beside them try to pinpoint as clearly as possible what is at the heart of what you love about them.

Movies: Heart:

Shows: Heart:

Color: Heart:

Item of clothing: Heart:

Weather: Heart:

Works of visual art: Heart:

Music: Heart:

Time in history: Heart:

Example (these are my husband's answers):

Movie: *The Godfather* trilogy   Heart: family, loyalty, tradition

Shows: *The Sopranos*   Heart: having a tribe

Color: green   Heart: nature

Item of clothing: fedora   Heart: sun protection, vintage things

Weather: rain   Heart: cosmic interruption

Works of visual art: anything with trees   Heart: heaven meets earth

Music: Dave Matthews Band   Heart: faith, joy, dance

Time in history: early America   Heart: revolutionary spirit, new ideas

Complete these prompts with the first thing that comes to mind:

I feel most like myself when I'm _painting_ and
swimming.
Heart: _O in the flow of art and nature_

To me, it is more important that someone is
accepting instead of _critical_.
Heart: _I grew up with vicious criticism._
My heart longs to feel complete acceptance

If I could snap my fingers and be anywhere in the world
right now, I would choose _Costa Rica_.
Heart: _Walk in ecological beauty,_
Country committed to peace; someplace I've
never been
It isn't fair when _people are judged by their weak-_
Heart: _My children_ _nesses instead of_
their strengths.

Everyone should _look into their own hearts,_
Heart: _____ _and know their own_
shadow.

I cannot stand it when someone says _____.
Heart: _____

It is so frustrating when _____.
Heart: _____.

What I really want is _____.
Heart: _____

I want people in my presence to feel _____.
Heart: _____

I want people who experience my art to know
_____.
Heart: _____

Example: It is so frustrating when *I am running late.*

Heart: Being late brings up feelings of being inconsiderate, unprepared, and living in chaos. When I say I want punctuality, what I mean is that I don't want to be rushed. I want to feel ready for whatever is happening next. I want more space and flexibility in my life.

Heart words: punctuality, readiness, space, flexibility. Write all the heart words and phrases from both parts of the exercise in one long list in your journal.

You may notice that some of your heart words, which in coaching we often call values, are in dissonance with one another. For example, punctuality is important to me, but so is flexibility. These things could be at odds in my life. (They often are, actually.) Having conflicting values is common and expected. As Walt Whitman says, "Do I contradict myself? Very well then, I contradict myself. I am large. I contain multitudes." Put a star beside any heart words that don't seem to go together. You can honor a particular value or not in each moment of your life.

One last read-through: take the heart words you settle on as most important to you and make sure they are precisely the right word. What does security mean to you? What do you mean when you say you value connection? Consider aspects of your personality that the prompts above may not have represented. What else is important to you? What other things do you value that are not reflected on this list?

Now take this list and create a simple work of art, a self-portrait. Try a medium that you do not usually use. Compose a song, write a poem, or take a selfie that captures something about you today. I had a coaching client create a word cloud with illustrations and another who made paper puppets, each one representing a different member of what we called her "inner team." Create your own artistic rendering of your heart words and display it somewhere you can see it. Where in your life are your values being honored? Which ones are being ignored? Where can you connect with others who hold similar values as you? Where can you most safely be yourself?

CODA ⊕

A woman named Araminta "Minty" Ross was born in Maryland around 1820. She was someone who *belonged* in the most horrific and tragic sense of the word. Born into slavery, she was the legal property of the Brodess family. Mr. Brodess had struck her in the head as a child, and after that injury, for the rest of her life, Minty experienced headaches, dizziness, fits, and spells—visions and dreams—the latter she believed were revelations from God. In her visions, Minty saw a world where she belonged only to God—a God who had created a world where she was free, where her loved ones were free.

When she was around thirty years old, she decided to escape to that world. She traveled with the help of the underground railroad all the way to Philadelphia, a journey of ninety miles. And it wasn't enough for her to save herself, although no one would have blamed her if she'd stopped there. She went back again and again into slave territory and worked as a conductor on the underground railroad, bringing dozens of enslaved Black people to freedom. Minty went by other names: her community called her Moses, after the prophet who led the Hebrews out of Egyptian slavery, and by a name you likely know—the name she chose as a free woman—Harriet Tubman.

Tubman would become the first woman to lead an armed expedition into war, during which she would free over seven hundred more enslaved people. After the war, she continued fighting for women's suffrage because her desire for this self-possession of belonging led her to see the world as it could be, not as it was.

It isn't enough for us to cross the border into a land of freedom for ourselves; we have to go back for our friends.

The legacy of Harriet Tubman reminds us that belonging is about more than finding your people. Her story shows us that once we experience true belonging, we can't help but want others to find it too. It isn't enough for us to cross the border into a land of freedom for ourselves; we have to go back for our friends. And this, by the way, does not mean we are all the same. No, it means we honor and celebrate each other's differences. And we use our voices to lift up those who have been silenced; we seek justice wherever we can. We work to make this place more like Harriet Tubman envisioned it could be, a world where no one is discarded or enslaved and where we are possessed by freedom. This type of belonging reminds us we are not free until we all are free.

Five True Things (don't forget to add yours):

1. Even if your biological family didn't support you, it doesn't mean you are not worthy of love and belonging.

2. "Belonging is belonging to myself first" (Brené Brown).

3. Being me is better than chasing after "normal."

4. "If you don't walk your true path, you don't find your true people" (Martha Beck).

5.

SEVEN

Ode to Reception
Your Work Is Not for Everyone, and That's Okay

"Overture," from *Nutcracker Ballet*,
by Pyotr Ilyich Tchaikovsky

Art's story then is not a trajectory of ascent, but more of a
looping spiral, constantly retracing its steps.
                        —Jonathan Jones, *The Guardian*, April 23, 2021

ROB

My friend Rob is known by everyone in his professional life as "The *Nutcracker* Conductor." He is the first call for orchestras and ballet companies everywhere. Not only as the music director of his own *Nutcracker* productions in different cities every year but also stepping in when someone falls ill or bows out at the last minute.

Recently, after the season ended (from November to January), I caught up with him and asked, "So, have you set a new record yet?" Previously the number of *Nutcracker* performances he had given in a single season was sixty.

He laughed, "Nope, but I can officially say I have the score memorized." (That's nearly two hours of music.)

My next question for him was maybe something you may also be wondering: "How do you stay inspired to do the same music night after night, year after year?"

"I'm always conducting for the one who is hearing the *Nutcracker* for the first or last time."

When creating for the masses, we miss the joy of the one.

INFINITY

"Ninety-nine . . . one hundred!" As I watched my little girl connect the numbers, eyes wide in wonder, she jumped on the couch with each gleefully squealed set until she suddenly stopped. With a very serious look, she said, "Mama, what comes after one hundred?"

Every artist uses a certain amount of mental space thinking about The Numbers. Once we have found the flow of making art, next comes sharing it, which brings up a whole number of feelings, like a subtle dread or the treacherous cocktail of insecurity, perfectionism, and a crazy specific and difficult goal to be reached. It has a very middle-school popularity contest energy, doesn't it? Often, coaching clients will come in excited to share about their latest art show or a piece of work that they believe resonates with their audience, but they speak with a certain sense of letdown in their voice. "Well, I only sold one piece," or "Only sixty people read that," or "I think I counted twenty folks in the audience last night." And because technology offers us more specificity than ever regarding the numbers of streams, clicks, downloads, and follows, we use that metric to measure our work's value, to tell us if it's good. And how could we not? Numbers are the very worst thing for a recovering perfectionist.

There's this story that Jesus told about the shepherd with one hundred sheep. It always perplexed me when I first heard it, around my daughter's age. The so-called good shepherd leaves the ninety-nine and goes after the one who had run away. Jesus says, "Who of you wouldn't run after the one until you can get him and bring him back?" Too timid to say it in Sunday school, I would hear that story and think, "No disrespect, but that seems majorly irresponsible, Jesus." Running after one sheep while the other ninety-nine are left to their own devices? Let the one go. Even back then, before the internet, I knew that having ninety-nine followers was better than having one.

What I had to tell my daughter, what I have to tell myself and my clients, is that after one hundred comes infinity.

MORE IS NOT ALWAYS BETTER

I often ask my clients (and myself): What number would be *enough*?

Rob, an atheist, would agree with Jesus. The good shepherd coming after the one sheep, Rob conducting for the little old lady or the young kid in the audience—this will turn your view of "enough" right on its head.

If we keep going down the obsessive counting path, not only do we miss out on the joy of each one, but we will also find ourselves full of despair. Funny how when we reach some goal or prescribed metric, the bar has a pesky way of moving. We finally learn how to count to one hundred as a four-year-old and realize there are just more numbers after that until your legs are much too tired to jump on the couch anymore.

Our culture is obsessed with moving the graph up and to the right, is it not? We do one thing and instantly begin feeling pulled toward more. We find some success, and people ask (or we ask ourselves), "What's next?" Do we open a storefront? Do we hire another person? Do we branch out into this or that market? Do we have another baby? Now that we have a Grammy, what about an Emmy, Tony, and an Oscar?

We swim in the soup that more is always better: but what if it isn't? What if this relentless pursuit of more is one of the reasons why you aren't writing the book or have lost inspiration in the work? Maybe you are too busy obsessing about your age or weight, about whether or not you're too—insert something you believe here—for this or that. You waste valuable mental space on projects that they tell you will lead to growth when you really want to stop here a moment and breathe. Or what about investing in those readers or audience members already there? Maybe you need to write that thing that your agent says no one will buy. Maybe instead of going after the one, you are trying to build a flock of thousands, but for what purpose and at what cost? Maybe you are disappointed when you look out into the audience and don't see a full house, all the while missing the little old lady in the back row weeping with joy for this chance to hear the music again. What if *one* is enough?

> *We swim in the soup that more is always better: but what if it isn't?*

FOR THE ONE WHO NEEDS TO HEAR THIS

You are more than a number, more than a sum of *yous.* You are not the means to an end in my getting the next book published or album recorded. Your creative work is worthy of being shared even if The Numbers tell a different story.

Thank you for being *my* one.

Because when I think of you holding this book, if you've gotten this far, having the privilege to speak into your life is enough for me. And remember, even when my work resonates with no other besides me, I can be the one that this is for.

When I shift to creating for my one—for Joshua, for Lauren, for Rebe—or the one whose daughter has cancer and the one who just quit her full-time job to start her own business or that one who just started making stuff again after a long hiatus—my mind shifts, my work shifts. These are names and details of real ones who I know will read this, and when I think of them, my cup runneth over with joy. Making for one humbles me, connects me with what matters most. It stops the chatter of the soulless perfectionist who could count the calories until she's a size zero but is just afraid of not being enough.

Go ahead and release yourself with this freeing statement: my work is not for everyone, and that's ok.

My work is not for everyone, and that's ok.

Your work is worth doing even if you are the only one who hears it or finds it meaningful. That work for you may be the thing you have to make or do to break through in a way you cannot see now. When you create for one, it dismisses the need to please everyone. Then when one or seven or ninety-nine people give you a less-than-stellar review or reject your submission, it will sting, but it won't tear you down because it was never about them. It was about the one that it was for. And that one is so precious, so worth creating for, so worth coming after.

Now, I realize to be an artist in the world, you must play the numbers game sometimes. We need the number in the bank account to be positive instead of negative. We want mainstream success. We want to publish the book traditionally, accrue millions of streams, and have our work featured in this or that place. We can want and need those things, but we mustn't give our numbers any more power over our feelings of worthiness. (We will discuss this directly in chapter 13.) When we create for the critic or for the masses, we miss the one who needs it most, and we can lose our joy.

Is your work a megaphone or an invitation?

Is your work a megaphone or an invitation?

Are you making stuff so you can collect likes or email addresses, or are you doing it because you have something you must say to someone out there who you think might need to hear it?

We can't let it stop us from going after the one.

THIS ONE'S FOR YOU

Like an albeit somewhat reckless, yet good, shepherd, I'll leave the ninety-nine and come for you. Like Rob, I'll play for the one hearing it for the first or last time. I'll see each and every person I play or write for as potentially the one. I won't stop creating for you, whoever you are. Just like the number on the scale is one tool you can use to determine health, the numbers in our creative life are just one way we measure progress. And just as you would never use a run-of-the-mill bathroom scale to measure how much you love someone, you can't use the numbers in your creative life to measure your value or impact. "To the world, you are just one person, but to one person, you may be the world," as the saying, often attributed to Dr. Seuss, goes.

There is someone who needs what you are making; they have lost hope and have stopped believing life matters anymore. Make it for them. You may never know their name or their circumstances. It could be centuries later, in a cold dark dusty library on some other planet, that it reaches the one it is for. No analytic or statistic can quantify how art reaches past infinity, our creative connection across time and space.

And don't forget that the one could be you.

SELF-COACHING QUESTIONS

1. What fears do you have about your creative work's reception in the world?

2. What numbers are you trying to reach? What number will feel like enough?

3. Where in your life have you been attempting to move up and to the right?

4. Look at the Jonathan Jones quote at the beginning of this chapter. Have you witnessed the "looping spiral" of art in your lifetime? Where have you seen art's story retracing its steps?

5. Who connects you to or reminds you of all the ones you are creating for?

ÉTUDE: THE ONE

Take a work of art you have finished, have recently performed, or something you are currently working on.

Who is the one that this work was/is for?

Fill in this profile below, envisioning the one.

(If the work of art is for you, fill it in with information about you. If a real-life one does not exist yet, dream about who they might be.)

Title of work of art:

Name of the one whom it is for:

Age:

Hometown:

Current location:

Emotional state before experiencing the art:

Emotional state during the art:

Emotional state after the art:

Struggles:

Joys:

The work of art helps them feel:

The work of art invites them to:

Lasting impact of the work of art on their life:

You may feel silly about making up these details about your reader/audience member if you don't know them, but in my experience the truth of the impact that your work has on the ones that it is for is far more interesting and meaningful than anything we could imagine. This process is meant to remind you of how your work ripples across time. You may not see its impact yet . . . or ever. Don't let that stop you creating for the one. They are worth coming after.

CODA ⊕

On September 12, 1940, eighteen-year-old Marcel Ravidah was walking his dog Robot near his home in southwestern France. Robot fell into a hole. Marcel ran and grabbed some friends to help rescue his beloved dog. He and his friends went down into the hole, and when they did, they discovered a cave full of incredible paintings. What we now know as Lascaux are 15,000–17,000-year-old cave paintings done during the Stone Age. The animals in the famous Hall of the Bulls were drawn in profile, making it appear that one mighty animal is looking right at you. These cave painters were highly experienced artists who understood perspective, craft, and expertise. When the caves were opened to the public some years later, one legend goes that Pablo Picasso himself viewed them and is rumored to have exclaimed, "They have invented everything." The veracity of these stories of Picasso has been challenged by some, but one thing is for sure: the cave paintings do share in what we call the cubist or modernist style of Picasso and others. Somehow, the artist or artists who painted Lascaux used a style that Picasso dabbled in in the early twentieth century. Picasso used the same style as Stone Age artists from 17,000 years ago.

Will you wait 17,000 years for the one? What if our metaphorical cave paintings are there not to help us climb the ladder to success, to ascend to heights of greatness, but to help us circle back, to remind those that see them seventeen millennia later that they're on the right track, that they aren't alone, that they have invented nothing, but also that we are all connected.

What would it do to your mindset or your mood to stop striving for the up and to the right and instead fall down the hole with Robot and let all that is right

What if our metaphorical cave paintings are there not to help us climb the ladder to success, to ascend to heights of greatness, but to help us circle back, to remind those that see them seventeen millennia later that they're on the right track, that they aren't alone, that they have invented nothing, but also that we are all connected.

in front of you or under your feet truly amaze you? Let the one you are creating for or with amaze you.

The Lascaux caves have now been closed to the public because too many human visitors were making them deteriorate more quickly. And that's a good lesson: may you protect your creative offerings from the numbers and know, regardless of who may or may not see them, they can still communicate across time. They do that thing that art does—as Jonathan Jones says—it connects us in that beautiful "looping spiral" of oneness.

Five True Things (you add the final one!):

1. My work is not for everyone, and that's okay.

2. The person who rejects my work doesn't get to define my work.

3. The power of my creations extends beyond my lifetime.

4. I will not put my value or mood in the hands of an audience member.

5.

EIGHT

Ode to Resilience
Where the Failures and Rejections Lead

Daphnis et Chloé Suite, No. 2, by Maurice Ravel

Thick Skin, Tender Heart.
>   —Rachel Held Evans, *Wholehearted Faith*

SARA

If they had given superlatives at music school, Sara would have been named "most likely to win a big audition." In truth, I didn't know her that well because while most of us were at post-concert parties, she was always practicing. But then I'd sit beside her in the orchestra while we played Ravel's *Daphnis et Chloe* and her sound bore a hole in my soul. There was a core to it, a strength, but gentleness, too. When we graduated, I watched her career, and for years she pounded the pavement to every single audition: Cincinnati, Boston, Chicago, San Diego, and Kansas City. Only a few flute chairs in orchestras came up every year, and if there was an audition, Sara was there. All told, she tried out for thirty different orchestras and made the final round of five of them.

Finally, on her thirty-first audition, she won; a second flute position in a reputable orchestra in a fairly large city. All that stood between her and the life of her dreams was getting tenure.

At the end of rehearsal, the week of her tenure review interview, the music director pulled her aside and asked to speak with her. She followed him into a dressing room. Two committee members were there when she walked in, waiting with solemn faces. "Sara . . . we are so sorry." She told me later that she couldn't hear anything they said after that. She couldn't remember how she'd gotten home from rehearsal, what she did next, or much of the days that followed.

In the face of failure, we must consider what lies within us more than what is behind or before.

WHAT I HAVEN'T TOLD YOU ABOUT NEW YORK

Somehow, God seemed to have forgotten the deal we'd made.

If I could go back to 65th Street on that day of my Juilliard graduation, the first day of the rest of my life, I wish I could pull that girl aside and tell her, "This next part is going to suck." The timing of failure can be one of those things that makes or breaks creative recovery. I've seen it happen to others; when faced with failure, while we also happen to be majorly burnt out, the two become a bitter cocktail of block.

When considering applying to Juilliard, I hadn't entered a religious establishment in years. I wouldn't have even considered myself a person of any faith at that moment, and yet when I stared at my uncertain future after my master's degree, I went searching for meaning, and I started to sense a new type of cosmic benevolence. I felt the urge to be brave, risk rejection and failure, take the leap, and apply to my dream school in my dream city.

The strength to do that didn't feel like it had come from me. The doors had opened, so I saw that as confirmation that the Heavens were shining on me. It was "God's Will" that I go to Juilliard and be a big success. What could go wrong? (I hope you are catching my sarcasm.)

What I haven't told you about that graduation day was that I had just applied to every job in all five boroughs and the tri-state area. I threw my hat in the ring for everything that I was even remotely qualified for (and a few I was not). And here's the thing—I got rejected by every. single. one. The playing gigs, the arts administration jobs, the basic paper-pusher nine-to-fives, even the hustles I most definitely did not want. When I stood there at my graduation and said to myself, "I don't know how I am going to do this for the rest of my life," I was also thinking, "They apparently aren't going to *let me* do this for the rest of my life, even if I wanted to."

NYC was ejecting me. Frank Sinatra said, "If I can make it there, I'll make it anywhere." The verdict was in; I could indeed not make it there. No job, no money, no apartment. The relationship I had spent years cultivating with someone I had thought I would marry fell apart. In months, the life I was barely holding together disintegrated as if it had never existed. This was a faith-altering failure. I felt everything from rancid bitterness to deep apathy.

As easy as God had made way for me to be there, the blessing was revoked like we'd reached the end of the rental agreement.

HOW TO FAIL WELL

When standing inside our own stories, failure blinds our vision like blood after a blow to the eyeball. Paralyzing, shame-inducing anger alternating with numbness; when artists fail, it can feel like the secret confirmation we've been expecting all along. *See? I knew I wasn't good enough. I knew that teacher was right. I knew I couldn't do it.* We give these moments power they should never have over us—one failed audition (or thirty), each public or even private rejection—they give us more information about ourselves than any success ever does. If we succeed, we have somehow pulled off a great heist and fooled everyone, and when we fail, we confirm our lack.

Learning how to rebound from failure (and yes, it is something you can learn) is central to creative recovery. In this chapter, the coaching questions and étude will be interwoven into the text. When you find yourself inside a failure, follow these three steps to rebound. Ask yourself these coaching questions and complete the practices when you feel ready.

> *Learning how to rebound from failure (and yes, it is something you can learn) is central to creative recovery.*

NO. 1: GRIEVE

So I had no choice but to move on from New York to the wild beyond. First to Chicago and then other cities, I built the plane while flying, trying to outrun my shame and sadness while attempting to appear like everything was fine. It was years before I could even enjoy being back in the Big Apple. The sense of rejection, plus the bitter pill of jealousy for "those people" who had gotten to stay, cast a long shadow on a place I used to love. I had yet to understand all that I had lost.

The first step to facing failure is to attempt to do that. To name what you've lost and to grieve it. Queen

Elizabeth II said, "Grief is the price we pay for love." So, pay up by paying attention to your grief. Make space in your life to admit to yourself the pain you are feeling. Go to therapy and lay it all out. Write it down and burn the list in your backyard. Cry. Talk to people who can listen to all your feelings, even the ugly and angry ones.

When that relationship ended, for example, you not only lost the person you thought you'd marry but also their entire family, the whole future that you'd imagined by that person's side is gone. Grieve it. You are surely better off in the long run, but when you are grieving, resist the temptation to put a pretty bow on it.

When you didn't get that job, you lost the office, the health insurance, the security, the respect, and the higher pay. When you didn't win that audition, you not only didn't get the gig but also had to continue worrying about what you would do next and how you would pay the rent. Let yourself feel all of that, give it a voice, and do not run from it. Numbing out with substances or more work can feel helpful in the short term for coping, but grief is the price we pay for love, and love is not cheap. We are sad because we cared, we hoped, and we loved. And it did matter. It was real and painful. Give in to the grief in meaningful ways, with the help of a loved one, counselor, or spiritual director.

SELF-COACHING QUESTIONS

1. What needs to be grieved?
2. What action can you take or ritual can you try to give time and attention to your grief process?

ÉTUDE: CREATE A RITUAL
TO PROCESS YOUR GRIEF

Rituals help us make sense of the world, express our feelings, and experience connection to others around us. What physical action can you take to be present to your pain or sadness?

Example: I read about one writer, Dheepa R. Maturi, who bought a bag of beads that looked like pearls and diamonds and, with each rejection, she put one in a clear dish on her writing desk. She believed the pressure of the writing life was creating something beautiful in her.

NO. 2: READ THE MAP

I have followed many feelings, many places, some helpful, others harmful. Julia Cameron, Harriet Lerner, and others have discussed feelings as maps. Asking the question: "What is my jealousy telling me?" can be powerful. What is your anger showing you about your boundaries, about what is important to you? And so maybe failure can be a map too. Once we've grieved, what information can be found in this loss?

What was the fact that I didn't get any of those jobs in New York saying about me? Some of those truths were hard, and others were quite helpful in helping me determine where I should go next. For some jobs I applied for, I just wasn't qualified. One job I was a perfect fit for resumé-wise, but (I later learned) it was given to someone else because of nepotism. A playing gig I wanted didn't pan out because they chose someone else who was very good. My relationship had failed because we had irreconcilable differences. The truth can set you free after you mourn and grieve the loss, to be sure. But there is information there for you if you can find it, and when you are ready.

The truth can set you free after you mourn and grieve the loss, to be sure. But there is information there for you if you can find it, and when you are ready.

Sometimes it means swallowing big pills about how you've contributed to your own failure. Sometimes it maps out the only path toward letting go, which is agreeing to disagree. The quote "A map is the greatest of all epic poems. Its lines and colors show the realization of great dreams" is often attributed to the founding editor of National Geographic, Gilbert H. Grosvenor. Learn to love your map and see even the treacherous terrain as an epic poem that is your life. When the grief and disorientation have passed, collect yourself and take stock of where the map of your life is leading you and what your failure means in the grand scheme. Ask yourself which parts of it you can control and which parts you are willing to attempt to control. (Just because you believe something is in control doesn't mean it is or should be managed by you.) Stop for a moment when you are done grieving, and read the map with patience and compassion. Do not let these steps delay you too long from continuing to walk your own unique path.

SELF-COACHING QUESTIONS

1. What direction is this failure pointing you toward? Is this the direction you want to go?

2. Where does the failure reveal your values, deepest longings, and weaknesses? What will you do with that

information? Return to your heart words in chapter 6. Which values need honoring now?

3. What can you control, and what can't you control? In what ways were you wrong? In what ways were you right?

ÉTUDE: RETROSPECTIVE MAP READING

It is often easier to read the map in hindsight. Remember a time when you failed in your past. Starting from the year and month you failed, write a short timeline of the steps you took next and how you arrived at the present day. What were you learning about yourself in the process of rebounding?

Example (based on true events):

September: Mona reached the end of an undergraduate degree in cello and decided she wanted to continue studying.

April: She was not accepted to a single graduate program of the ten she applied to.

June: She moved back in with her parents for the summer and decided to take a month off from playing to regroup.

July: Her father was a professor at a medical school in her hometown, and at his suggestion, she decided to enroll in a biology course at the community college.

September: She got a job teaching young kids at a local music school, played cello gigs, and took other pre-med classes.

Two years later: She enrolled in medical school. She cofounded the medical student orchestra.

Today: Mona is a neurology resident studying the effects of music on the brain. She still plays cello in a part-time community orchestra.

The map can be hard to read when we are inside our failures, big or small. The fact that Mona found a career she loved doesn't take away the sting she felt from not being able to go to the graduate school of her dreams. It took her years to unravel all of it. But in the end, she let the failure lead her to the next place she was supposed to go. She grieved. She surrounded herself with people who loved and knew her; she listened to her life. She kept moving and let the rejection of all those graduate programs teach her the lesson she was meant to learn.

NO. 3: KNOW THAT WE ARE MORE THAN WHAT WE DO

The grieving period may be long, especially if you equate your identity with your creative work. For Sara, that was the heart of it.

Once Sara finished the horrific season sitting in an orchestra that did not offer her tenure, she too went home to live with her parents for a while. You could say she disappeared from public life. If her failure was a map, that life experience was an atomic bomb that decimated the landscape in one blow. Her usually optimistic disposition had been replaced by a blankness that concerned her closest loved ones; she wasn't sure who she was.

After a few weeks of barely leaving the house or her bed, her mother suggested she get some help, so she checked herself into an inpatient psychiatric care center. She told me that when the thought of taking her own life was the only thing giving her energy, she knew it was time. She said she was so grateful for the lifeline of the doctors and therapists who helped her during the three months she spent in recovery there, and when it was time for her to leave, she asked her mom to bring her flute. She played a short, simple melody for them as a goodbye gift. Even though she was out of practice, she said it was the only way she knew how to share her gratitude to the community that had given her her life back. When we last spoke, she was playing here and there as a substitute, considering returning to the audition circuit. No one except her closest loved ones knew she had been in treatment.

Like all the stories in this book, Sara's is based on a real person. I'm sharing her failure with you because she told me that three months without her flute in an inpatient psychiatric treatment center had taught her what she had all but forgotten: she was more than a flutist. She had spent so much time cultivating her flute player identity that she had forgotten all about who she was without it, so she felt irrevocably lost when it was stripped away.

It feels important to say here that, as spiritual as I am, one thing I do not believe is that everything happens for a reason. I am not asking you to take your greatest places of pain and throw some toxic positivity on them, buck up, and call it a day. Sometimes you really should have gotten tenure. Sometimes you were the most talented person there. Sometimes life is not fair. Naming what you learn from the failure is different from saying you are glad it happened. That is why we grieve first. Some things

Naming what you learn from the failure is different from saying you are glad it happened. That is why we grieve first. Some things happen for no reason at all. It is painful. And yet, I believe that the things that happen to us can ultimately be used for our good. They can make us stronger, more compassionate, humble, and resilient if we choose to do the hard work of letting them.

happen for no reason at all. It is painful. And yet, I believe that the things that happen to us can ultimately be used for our good. They can make us stronger, more compassionate, humble, and resilient if we choose to do the hard work of letting them.

There is zero shame in getting help. If you are experiencing dark thoughts, do not believe their lies that your life has no value or we'd be better off without you. Pick up the phone and call someone—a friend, a therapist, or a suicide prevention hotline. You're not alone. This, too, shall pass.

Even when you feel like the bomb of failure has destroyed everything, grieve, rest, get help when needed, and then stand up and look around. No failure can take away your identity. You are more than what you do.

Cultivate a sense of self-worth outside of what you do or make. Learn to love yourself despite your successes and failures. It isn't about being perfect or acceptable or successful, it's about offering yourself unconditional compassion no matter what creative challenges you face.

SELF-COACHING QUESTIONS

1. Return again to your heart words in chapter 6. Who are you outside of your creative performance?

2. Review the self-care needs from chapter 2. How are you doing with taking care of the creative instrument that is you? Double down on self-care when you fail.

3. Who can help you grieve and process the failure? Who can help you read the map by offering some much-needed perspective?

ÉTUDE: "DEAR ME" LETTER

Write a letter of condolence to yourself when you feel rejected or face failure. In the letter, be as specific as possible, reminding yourself of your strength and resilience. Name a few things you love about yourself, especially those unrelated to your creative expression. Say all the things you long to hear. Read the letter out loud to yourself in the mirror.

CONGRATULATIONS, YOU FAILED

The bottom line: you cannot let one audition, failed marriage, or royal screw-up (or a string of them) define you, because they are not you. You are more complex and eternal than some failure or success could ever get at. When you believe in your own worthiness, uniqueness, and beauty, regardless of where you work or who gave you tenure, then, when failure comes, it will not decimate your land. It can hurt and grieve you deeply, but it won't destroy you.

Failure and rejection are inevitable if you live with courage and take the risks your goals require. When I am rejected, my writing coach, Ann Kroeker, always says something like, "Congratulations, you're doing the work of a writer." And you and I both are so much more than that work.

Failure and rejection are inevitable if you live with courage and take the risks your goals require.

Your life has value if you never win an audition or if everyone unsubscribes or unfollows, if you never book another gig—you are beloved. Grieve your loss, explore what it can teach you, and do the work to love yourself regardless (or despite) your failures and achievements.

CODA ⊕

A young athlete trained to be an Olympic figure skater from childhood, and her first major failure came by way of the 1986 US Olympics when, after all that work, she didn't make the team. She pivoted to her second love—fashion—and amazingly wound up as an editor at *Vogue* magazine. But failure was not done with her yet. She left *Vogue* after being brushed off for the editor-in-chief position. At age forty, she wondered what was next.

She got engaged at age thirty-nine and could not find a wedding dress she liked. Her businessman father saw this as an opportunity, so he encouraged her to open her own bridal store. Eventually, she started sketching wedding gowns of her own design. Those sketches became a fashion empire worth more than $1 billion.

That figure skating failure was none other than Vera Wang.

When you've grieved your losses, will you see there is hope to be found in what is coming next? And don't worry if you can't see it yet.

What if you believed that the simple act of picking up a pencil and sketching a dream could lead to your next passion project? How did Vera Wang's figure skating past or failed attempts to make editor play into her success? How did all this make her especially qualified to design? Regardless of what horrific failures you've seen in your day, no matter the embarrassment or shame that you've experienced within them, it is never too late to pick yourself up and keep moving forward through every twist and turn. You never know what could come next. What if, beyond the grief, there was opportunity and hope, but only when we love ourselves enough to keep going?

Five True Things (don't forget to add yours):

1. Nothing that is truly yours can be missed.
2. "Failure is not the opposite of success. It is part of success" (Stephen Hawking).
3. When you fail, double down on self-care.
4. You were made to do remarkable things.
5.

NINE

Ode to Feedback

Stop Listening to People You Don't Even Like

"There Is a Balm in Gilead," Spiritual, sung by Mahalia Jackson

You keep listening to those who seem to reject you. But they never speak about you. They speak about their own limitations. The sadness is that you perceive their necessary withdrawal as a rejection of you instead of as a call to return home and discover there your true belovedness.

—Henri J. M. Nouwen, *The Inner Voice of Love*

OLIVE

She draped her body in flowy shirts and colorful prints as if nothing was wrong, but she felt like a warzone in a pashmina. Six months after the double mastectomy, she still had a hard time recognizing herself in the mirror.

This was one of the main reasons she had signed up for our creative recovery group. The dysmorphia was especially perplexing to Olive because, as a visual artist who taught life drawing at a local community arts center, she was intimately acquainted with and accepting of the human form, even her own. She'd posed nude countless times in art school with zero insecurity. She had not only spent hours memorizing curves and bends of elbows, but she had also lovingly and carefully recreated these bodies with charcoals and sold them for money. Not recognizing or accepting her own form now felt like a deep betrayal.

Our group ended with no large revelation for Olive (as far as I knew). One of the other group members, Marjorie, was also an art teacher in a city nearby, and when Olive shared how this disconnect with her body was bothering her, it gave Marjorie an idea. She asked Olive, timidly at first, if she would be open to posing for one of her classes. "I think it might help, Olive. Let these artists help you see yourself." Olive was wondering if this invitation was a sign of synchronicity; unsure as she was about it, she said yes.

As she undressed and found a pose that felt natural, surrounded by a handful of eager artists that Marjorie had organized—all women—she noticed her hands were shaking. She looked down at her sun-spotted arms and her scarred chest. Suddenly she felt grateful to be alive. Unbeknownst to Olive, these women drawing her had also struggled to accept and love their bodies; many were cancer survivors. The room fell silent. Olive felt that familiar combination of strength and vulnerability rush over her.

Sometimes we can only see ourselves clearly when we let the right people in.

THE EXISTENTIAL QUESTION

Once upon a time, after I played a recital, a man got down on one knee during the curtain call and proposed marriage to me in front of everybody. I was happy at that moment, if a little surprised. With his question came so many of my own.

> Where would we live? (We had jobs halfway across the country from each other.)
>
> Would this last? (We had broken up before.)
>
> Did I want to spend the rest of my life with him?

As happy as I was, I cannot recall another decision that put me more at odds with myself or one that seemed to subject me to more public scrutiny. My teachers and mentors had set the example: at all costs, put your career first. Put it before any man or any child or anything else in life that you may want— because getting a job as an oboist was all there was to be or do.

And up to that point, I had done that. For me, that meant moving around and ending relationships when they became incompatible with my career plans. It meant not stopping to think too hard about whether the place I was going to be an oboist was somewhere I wanted to be or not.

And after the "New York Failure," I felt lucky to have a job. I believed that if I just had my own office with a grand piano or my name on the door, if I had somewhere to hang my newly framed diplomas, then I'd, of course, be happy because what else is there for me? In this job, I had all that, plus health insurance. And the fact that it was a nine-hour drive away from the person I was dating notwithstanding, it was going quite well.

I loved the idea of marrying him, but I also loved my work, and most of all, I loved all the things I believed having *that* job meant about me.

As he kneeled there, hands shaking and brow dripping sweat onto his velvet blazer, it felt like he was asking me something I had been afraid to ask myself about my priorities, my worthiness. Marry him and everything would shift.

When people propose to us, when life makes us an offer we can't refuse, I've watched many artists I coach ask the same existential question I was asking myself in the face of the ring that day.

What will everybody think?

A PEOPLE PLEASER'S NIGHTMARE

In her book *Finding Your North Star*, sociologist Martha Beck explores this idea of "Everybody" or what sociologists call "the generalized other." She believes that every person has their Everybody: the committee of people who seem to uphold the impossible personal, moral, and professional standards, the arbiters of how each of us should behave.

To find out who your Everybody is, Beck suggests finishing the following sentences "People judge me because . . ." or "Society keeps telling me I have to . . ." and then try to come up with as many real-life people that hold that judgmental opinion as you can. Beck explains that when her clients give real names and faces to their generalized other, they can't always find more than one or two people who believe those things. One or two judgmental people loom that large in our minds. And here's the worst part, according to Beck: The real people who comprise our Everybody are most often the ones who have discounted our truest selves.

In other words, this Everybody is the minority, not the majority. They are the last people we should ask to judge our decisions because, in many cases, they are people we do not even like.

It was like that proposal had given my inner artist-child a voice that had long been drowned out by all the loud judgmental yelling of people I was trying to please. It was like he had snuck up to my inner me and quietly asked her if she wanted to go on the adventure of a lifetime, and all I had to do was convince my grown-up, people-pleasing self to set her free to go.

I wish I could say I came to that decision in strength and power, that once I heard that voice, I trusted it and followed it immediately, but it was wrought with many months of tears and intense anxiety. I would lie awake thinking, "Everybody will think I'm crazy if I leave a full-time job! The people that hired me are going to blacklist me forever for leaving after two years! They are going to say I am not a feminist, following my husband around! This will mar my resumé forever; I'll never get a job like this again. Everybody is going to hate me. This is *not* something you do."

THE FEEDBACK LOOP

The hardest part for creatives when naming and examining the generalized other is that when we share our work, we get feedback and messages from all kinds of people all the time. They unabashedly praise or constructively criticize or verbally attack our art, which, good or bad, feels personal. From trusted mentors and friends to faceless internet trolls, it can be hard to differentiate ourselves from what we create and how we perceive others' reactions to it.

We are put in positions to receive feedback from people we do not know at all (like a competition panel) or from someone we do know and certainly do not respect or admire, like the toxic teacher who holds the key to your future as an artist or performer. And these poisonous playmates (as Julia Cameron calls them) can have the knowledge, expertise, and talent we need to excel and improve. Outsiders would have us believe we are lucky to be allowed in their presence while holding our instrument. Yet, the methods they use to motivate, correct, or otherwise help you acquire more artistic skills can be harmful. The feedback loop for the artist is an echo chamber of confusing and emotional cacophony. We long for confirmation that we are ok and will go to great lengths to receive it.

The feedback loop for the artist is an echo chamber of confusing and emotional cacophony. We long for confirmation that we are ok and will go to great lengths to receive it.

If the abuse or shaming is something you believe is required of you in the name of being a great artist, please know—that is a lie. Report it to someone you trust. Do not give this person power over you for one more minute. Under no circumstances should your creative development chip away at your personhood. It is possible to hone your selective hearing for critical feedback (more ear-training, imagine that), to distill the words down to something helpful, and to leave the rest. That starts with the difficult work of naming a supportive, helpful, loving Everybody for yourself.

Even when we finish school, after we release ourselves from these toxic teachers or put years in between us and the haters' harmful words, they can slip into our Everybody without noticing. In some cases, we let their judgments, the things they said to us fifteen or twenty years ago, speak into other decisions they have no business being part of. The critical voices reverberate louder than the positive ones.

That is, until we work to change that.

FINDING THE RIGHT EVERYBODY

I listened to Martha Beck's book while driving the nine-hour trip back and forth to that man who proposed to me, attempting to make the hardest decision of my life up to that point. After months of trying to find work for him in my city, nothing was panning out. Since his job was within driving distance of multiple major metropolitan areas where I had contacts, he was confident I would find work there. We had long conversations that were wrought with emotion. Somewhere on I-95, I slammed head-first into my Everybody.

I realized it was made up of people who did not understand or know me. And don't get me wrong, some of them have names; a colleague told me to my face that I was setting a bad example for female students, leaving a job for a man. A mentor told me I would likely end up divorced, that I would never get another job like this again. These were hard things to hear, but they were by no means the majority.

Why do we give such weight to the words of unsupportive and sometimes downright hateful people? Why do we remember word-for-word the harmful searing criticism of that review but can't recall the heartfelt comments from those we love the most? You get to make your generalized other a very specific and curated team of people who support you. You can decide whose opinions matter to you and whose don't. You can read the comments or not.

people who support you. You can decide whose opinions matter to you and whose don't. You can read the comments or not.

I decided that my Everybody would be carefully chosen close friends, some family, and a mentor that I trust. This Everybody supports my inner life over my professional one; they nurture my creative self as it is unfolding. They know that one of the reasons I got so burnt out after New York was because I had failed to listen to my life speak. And lest you think it is a circle of compliments always padding my ego, this Everybody lets me know when I'm wrong. We disagree sometimes. Their feedback can sting, but they never use shame to motivate me. That is what being loved and accepted feels like. Living your life to please others will leave you anxious, lonely, empty, and burnt out; been there, done that.

GO DISAPPOINT SOMEONE TODAY

So, who is your Everybody? Maybe it's your overbearing parent or that frenemy from college. Maybe it's an institution or group whose ideals you no longer uphold or believe. Maybe it is people that you do not even like or enjoy being around. Do not give that Everybody power over your life for one more second. Do the hard work of self-discovery and exercising your agency, be brave about discovering what is best for you, and do that regardless of whom you will disappoint.

I knew a therapist who used to say, "Do not pick up what is not yours to carry." Through the work of creative recovery, I've learned that most hateful people have a terrible and abusive Everybody. Picking up anybody else's baggage continues the cycle of pain. It weighs us down and keeps us blocked. Being a joyful artist means not taking everything personally. It means being strong enough to be a self-actualized human in a world of insecure, broken people who say, "Here. Hold this."

I said yes that day, to Edwin, and I have never once looked back. And I realize the privilege that was afforded me to win and then quit a full-time job in the first place, to have a spouse with a career who could support me financially while I found more work I loved. This was the best decision for our family. I hope it will inspire you to do whatever is right for you and yours without fear of what Everybody will think. I've seen many of my artist clients and friends not live in congruence with their deepest values in order to please people; they so often lose their creative joy.

If you are facing a difficult decision, one where someone or large groups of someones will be disappointed regardless of what you decide, I wouldn't dare tell you what to do except to try and relish the process of getting to the other side of the difficult decisions. Let all the feedback you allow yourself to absorb be from people you trust. Let the rest go. Whatever you do, do not give the wrong Everybody power over your life's choices. Life is too short to create for the critic.

WHAT IF EVERYBODY LOVES YOU

Olive took a break from modeling and browsed the artists' work. Her perceived imperfections, her scars, and her dimpled skin were portrayed in the light of strength and power by one artist. By another, she was demur and elegant; her body's gray and black lines were whimsical, angelic. She teared up. They had seen so much more than any mirror ever could; she realized that life in a body was enough to make it beautiful, and she began coming home to herself. That group of supportive women artists had given her that gift.

There are going to be decisions in your life that are hard. Feedback will come at you from all sides, especially when you bravely create things you care about. There will be crossroads, and no one is expecting you to go it alone. And yet, you don't have to stand naked in front of just any group of life-drawing artists. We get to choose our own Everybody. If your career as an artist, or any career, asks you to make sacrifices that go against what you truly want and long for, or if you aren't with someone who is fighting for you to thrive and flourish personally and professionally, no matter the money or the validation it gives you in the eyes of Everybody, these relationships are not worth it. Find your Everybody; imagine them as artists armed with sketchbooks, there to remind you who you are. Let the right Everybody call you home and, as Nouwen reminds us, rediscover your true belovedness.

SELF-COACHING QUESTIONS FOR WHEN YOU RECEIVE FEEDBACK

1. What can I learn about myself here?

2. Do I agree with this person's assessment of me? What parts of their feedback have some truth in them? What parts are categorically wrong?

3. Am I taking this personally? What other tender spots or creative wounds does this touch in me?

4. Do I know, respect, and admire this person criticizing me?

5. What boundaries do I need to set around when and how I receive feedback?

ÉTUDE: NAMING EVERYBODY

Inspired by Martha Beck's exercise in *Finding Your Own North Star: Claiming the Life You Were Meant to Live*.

List the top five most painful pieces of feedback you have ever received and the names of those who gave them.

List the top five most positive pieces of feedback you have ever received (could be a compliment or helpful constructive criticism) and the names of those who gave them.

If you can't think of five or remember names, leave them blank. Let the fact that you can't remember reveal the lasting impact it has had or hasn't had.

My Creative Everybody Committee:

In your journal, list the individuals whom you trust to give feedback and counsel on your creative endeavors.

Questions to ask before adding people to this list:

- Are they calling me toward my truest, most joyful, creative self, even when that means bucking the status quo?

- Do they have a conflict of interest? Meaning, if I behave or perform in a certain way, would it affect them in some way, positive or negative?

- Do I feel shame (less-than, somehow flawed) when I am in their presence?

- Do I respect and admire them?

- Are they in the ring, doing creative work themselves? Do I like or admire their art and their career?

My Personal Everybody Committee:

In your journal, list the individuals who you trust to give feedback and counsel on your personal life.

Questions to ask before adding people to this list:

1. Are they calling me toward my truest self, even when that means bucking the status quo?
2. Do they have a conflict of interest, meaning if I behave or perform a certain way would it affect them in some way, positive or negative?
3. Do I feel shame (less-than, somehow flawed) when I am in their presence?
4. Do they have a joyful, stable, fulfilling life?
5. Martha Beck: "If you had a baby and were forced to leave your child to be raised by other people, whom would you choose?"

If you have trouble listing more than one or two, that's okay. There is no designated number of Everybody committee members needed for a joyful life. What matters is your intentionality and awareness about whose feedback you absorb.

BONUS ÉTUDE: CREATE A SMILE FILE

Collect meaningful feedback (compliments or constructive criticism that help you) and put it somewhere on your computer or in a specific journal with the date and person's name. Work to hone your skill of discernment at all costs.

Keep returning to your Everybody committee lists, especially when you need to make big decisions or when someone's feedback stings. Look for the truth in whatever feedback you receive. Let the truth motivate you and call you home to your own belovedness through the people who know and love you.

CODA ⊕

On August 28, 1963, Rev. Dr. Martin Luther King Jr. walked to the podium on the steps of the Lincoln Memorial to deliver a speech to 250,000 civil rights supporters during the March on Washington. Bystanders reported that King seemed nervous. He usually spoke without a script, but that day he was looking down at his notes anxiously. At one moment, King hesitated, and it was then that the singer Mahalia Jackson shouted, "Tell them about the dream, Martin!"

Off script, he spoke from his heart one of the most memorable speeches made in American history. Historian Jon Meacham said, "With a single phrase, Martin Luther King Jr. joined . . . the ranks of men who've shaped modern America."

There were likely many people screaming in that crowd that day, and King had listened to Mahalia Jackson. He had taken her invitation to share the dream; he had let her words change the course of his speech, change the course of history.

Of those screaming from your audience, to whom will you be listening? Who are you allowing to change your course of action? I don't believe anyone who says they don't care what others think: if we are blind to others' opinions, we become narcissistic individualists who live only for ourselves.

Yet Dr. King knew when to allow others' opinions through; he knew which voices called him toward the dream and which did not. If you know anything about his life, you know it was far from easy to drown out the sound of that harmful Everybody. Yet he kept walking toward the dream in the face of violence, even death. Mahalia Jackson's voice calling from the crowd reminds us that some support our life's mission and some do not, that the choice is ours who we listen to.

Let us let Dr. King's life call us to fight for justice. Let it remind us to be bold in the face of whatever dissenters or naysayers we encounter. I dream that we stay open to influence by those who see the dream when we cannot, who call us into our truest selves, and who lead the way to a better world.

Five True Things (don't forget to add yours):

1.   It is unsustainable to take everything personally.

2.   I decide whose feedback I take to heart.

3.   When I do not live up to an expectation (internal or external), it does not mean I am a bad person or a bad artist.

4.   I will not pick up what is not mine to carry.

5.

TEN

Ode to Abundance
Creativity Is Tapas, Not Pie

"Allegro Molto Appassionato," from *Violin Concerto*, Op. 64,
by Felix Mendelssohn

You can't use up creativity. The more you use, the more you
have.

—Maya Angelou, interview with
Bell Telephone Magazine 61, no. 1 (1982)

ADELAIDE

There was something inhumane about performing
in an empty two-thousand-seater hall save for three
judges sitting in the fifteenth row. While in school,
she was one of thirty violinists from around the world
invited to a large competition. After she performed, she
felt relieved it was over and confident in how she'd done.
But in the otherwise empty hall, the three occupants of
row T were looking down and writing; the only energy
to pull from was their scrutiny and apparent boredom.
Regardless, Adelaide had tried to play with energy and
personality, to take chances even if it meant she didn't
execute things perfectly.

The finalists were announced at the end of the day, and now the previously empty auditorium was full of nervous energy and whispered conversations. Only the top three out of about thirty contestants would get to compete in the finalists' recital, which was the next day. If Adelaide didn't advance, she'd be free to leave. She stood in the back of the hall by the door when the proctor came to the podium. In her experience, it was best to make a speedy exit, whether you win or lose. When the announcer got to the names and Adelaide didn't hear hers, she felt shockingly numb. She took a deep breath and picked up her stuff and headed to the nearest exit. As she opened the door, the announcer added: "All contestants who would like to receive their comment sheets from the judges can collect them at the registration desk following this meeting." Adelaide immediately slipped out of the auditorium, made her way to the desk, and was the first one there. They handed her a thin manila envelope.

When she got to the car and opened the comments, she was shocked by two things:

1. How much each of the judges had written.

2. The fact that they had ranked each contestant and had included their ranking right there on the comment sheet.

Judge no. 1 had her ranked twentieth out of thirty. He did write "nice tone" early on, but then just fussed about her rhythm in the Mendelssohn concerto and her tempi in the Bach. He wrote nothing about the final piece.

Judge no. 2 had her ranked eighth out of thirty. He was very complimentary overall until the very last piece, "lovely interpretation and stage presence, love the tempos of the Bach!" Then his handwriting changed. He scribbled, "What happened???" (The question marks mocked her.) "The contemporary piece felt emotionless."

Judge no. 3 had ranked her first out of thirty. He had written her a letter. It said:

> Dear Adelaide, It is almost impossible to put into words how your performance impacted me today. We have heard many violinists play the same repertoire, and yours was the most engaging, meaningful, and polished rendition. All I can say in summary is: you've got it. I know we will be hearing great things from you in the future.

Then he signed his name.

EATING LIKE A SPANIARD

My husband Edwin and I have this perpetual disconnect about leftover food. If I leave a couple of bites of something on my plate, say a few French fries or a bite or two of chicken, as I go to scrape my plate into the compost or trash, he'll protest. "Hey, hey, let's wrap that up; I'll eat it later." Oh, the creativity with which that man manages the takeout leftovers!

He'll order us three entrées for two people, deeply enjoying a little of each dish. And when lunch comes around the next day, he'll throw the extra fries or the chicken from that other meal, plus an egg over-medium atop the shrimp fried rice or whatever (leaving three or four dirty Tupperware containers in the sink to be washed, mind you), but otherwise creating a delicious concoction that I did not see coming. When we first married, I was perplexed—okay, maybe a bit annoyed—by this, but it has become endearing. Meals with Edwin are a creative endeavor, a hodgepodge of flavors and textures.

When we traveled to Spain a few summers ago, visiting the land of my husband's ancestors, his favorite place on the globe, I finally understood his relationship to food. The thing that struck me most about eating in Spain was not the food itself per se, but the way Spaniards approached eating in general.

Take dinner, for example. In the summer, it stays light very late, in some places as late as 11:00 p.m. Dinner begins (at the earliest) at 9:00 p.m. The later in the day, the lighter the fare becomes (hence, the tapas idea). At the average Spanish restaurant at 11:00 p.m., you will see tables full of people sitting together late into the night enjoying a leisurely "meal." I put it in quotes because it goes on so long, and the food is so varied, that it feels more like never-ending appetizers. Eventually, everyone drinks coffee instead of wine, and the evening ends with a stroll in the plaza, not with that crazy-full American dinner feeling, but one of lightness, satisfaction, and laughter. The Spanish seem to savor just a few morsels of these curated dishes, each made with top ingredients, and the conversation and togetherness are like their own little tapas too. Watching Spaniards eat, slowly and surrounded by friends and family, the meal is just as much a social event as dinner. Many times, I thought we were done, and out came another dish. Edwin constantly reminded me to slow down, enjoy each bite, sit, and savor. In those moments, I was so grateful to be alive; eating in Spain was an act of gratitude and joy . . . even if it was after midnight before we finished.

Being the designated "creative" person in our household, sometimes it shocks me how I lack creativity in certain avenues of life. The kitchen is surely one, but parenting is another. At the center of creativity are freedom, fun, and possibility, and it shocks me how some of the most creative people I know, myself included, often choose predictability and seriousness instead. It's like we sequester creativity to the easel or the artmaking, ask that it exist only in certain arenas, and forget the power it might have to help us solve problems (like wasting food) or, at the very least, help us enjoy life a little more.

But maybe the reason I do not pull creative joy into my daily life is that right alongside my desire to create are feelings of jealousy, competition, and fear. Sometimes when I'm reading a great book or listening to a recording of music I love, I am ashamed to admit that my first feeling is not *Wow, what a beautiful expression of creativity!* No, if I am honest, I often feel awash with dread. *Ugh. I'm not good enough. I'm too late.* I go around and around in my head with thoughts of scarcity. *There are a finite number of words in the English language, and there are so many writers out there; why should I even try? Someone has already said it better, and they have one million followers, so what's the point?* And this kind of thinking does not lead me to feel more free, joyful, or creative. It makes me feel dejected, jealous, and fearful.

In my mind, creativity feels like a pie. With limited pieces, you better get one before they're gone. That kind of thinking makes us see the creative work of colleagues as a threat. We can't enjoy the process or great creative work of others because we're too busy being scrappy, trying to get ours. And it isn't completely our fault, is it?

For example, many artistic fields are extremely competitive, like Adelaide's violin world, for example. There are funders and funds, titles, and chairs in orchestras to be had, and sometimes there is no escaping competition and comparison.

But what if we could separate the business of creativity from the art of living a creative life? What if it could feel less like fighting for pie and more like eating Spanish tapas? Because what other choice do we have, really? The pie keeps getting smaller and smaller. The number of us wanting a piece keeps getting larger and larger; all the while, we are just more anxious and depressed and creatively dry.

There is always room for one more tapa, for one more friend at the table. The deliciousness of *jamón ibérico* does not take away from the exquisite salty/sweet combination of bacon-wrapped dates. The purpose of coming to the table is to find community and to be fed. When you show up hungry, you will get to eat, so you can stop comparing yourself to others. What if there was more than enough?

FROM THE STOMACH COMES THE DANCE

When Adelaide told me about her experience with the three judges who ranked her so differently in the same competition, I knew I wanted to share the story because it is proof of how we cannot give others the power to determine our creative worth. What if she'd never seen those comments? What if the one judge who had ranked her near the top hadn't shown up that day? What if she took the fact that she didn't advance to the finals to be the confirmation of the thing she'd feared most of all: "I guess I don't have what it takes." The only thing the competition confirmed was that those judges had wildly different musical opinions about her playing, which is only useful to Adelaide insofar as she agrees or disagrees with their opinions. So, a reminder: you can agree or disagree with others' opinions of your work. Being an artist with integrity and authenticity requires that of you.

The danger of comparing yourself to others is that you are tempted to become less of yourself in the process. Sometimes, your field of creative work pits you against certain other artists; sometimes, it's unavoidable. Whether or not you find yourself in one of these explicit competition situations where judgment is imminent, or if it's more subtle, and you feel yourself competing in the market with other artists vying for the same slice of pie, remember: There is space for everyone. But you can only claim your space and feed your soul if you

The danger of comparing yourself to others is that you are tempted to become less of yourself in the process.

stay true to your artistic vision. You must play the tempo you think the thing should go. Make the art the way you envision it. Don't write for the critic or the judge; write for the hungry, yourself among them. If you can't separate your vision from your mentor's or your fellow competitors', then retreat into yourself until you can see it, and seek it with gentleness and curiosity—What do I want to say here? What is moving me about this? How can I share my joy with my audience?

And when you read some critic's verdict, when you feel your head spinning like Adelaide did, reading those judges' comments in her car, consciously decide to investigate the open fridge and choose not to say, "There's nothing for dinner." Instead, be open to the joy of creating dinner out of a few pieces of cheese, some leftover meat, and some crackers. Throw in some fig jam and you've got yourself a tapa. Choose abundance when the world sees scarcity and utilize creativity as a tool to get you there. Let the joy of that process wash away the rancid bitterness of comparison and jealousy that will ruin any great meal.

There's a Spanish saying, *De la panza sale la danza*, which translates roughly to "from the stomach, comes the dance." It takes massive energy to keep up the sometimes difficult and vulnerable work that is putting our art out into the world. But Maya Angelou was right; the more creativity we use, the more we have. May we see the sustenance offered us when we choose gratitude and abundance. Creativity isn't pie; it is Spanish tapas. May we let it feed all who are hungry and fuel whatever dance we dance with joy.

Creativity isn't pie; it is Spanish tapas.

SELF-COACHING QUESTIONS

1. In what company or around which people do you feel most competitive?

2. What fears are behind your feelings of scarcity?

3. What areas of your life could benefit from creative problem solving?

4. Does competition motivate you or burn you out? What other feelings does it bring up?

5. Who are your biggest competitors? Have you reached out to them in friendship and community? What would that feel like?

ÉTUDE: LENS SHIFTING

Thinking of creativity like tapas instead of pie is, put simply, a shifting of the lens. This étude is adapted from "The Anatomy: The Foundational Coaching Course," created by Quinn Simpson and McKenzie Cerri, founders of Graydin. It allows you to state where you stand today and what stories you are telling yourself about your situation, and it offers a fun way to try on new lenses for seeing things differently to overcome creative block.

First, let's name your situation and current lens. Here are some questions to help you do that:

1. Choose one creative challenge you are facing right now. Write the facts about what you are experiencing without using any adjectives (descriptive words).

Example: Creative Challenge—I am editing my book. I spend three or four hours daily working on this project of 50,000+ words. It takes time, but it also takes energy.

(As you describe a challenge in this way, you'll start to notice that your situation is already so closely linked to the story you are telling yourself about it.)

2. Now write all the adjectives (descriptive words) that come up when you think of this challenge.

Example: hard, time-consuming, overwhelming, exhausting, seeming never to end, creatively draining.

3. Pick one lens that best describes the way you see your challenge.

Example: Current Lens—overwhelming.
Your Current Lens:

For this exercise, you will need three works of visual art (by someone besides you). They can truly be from any time period, medium, or style. I've given you some examples that you can do a quick internet search to view, but if you are sitting in a coffee shop or anywhere there are works of visual art, use those.

Examples:

> Picasso, *Girl in the Mirror*
> Sherald, *Portrait of Michelle Obama*
> Pollock, *Autumn Rhythm*

Take each of the paintings you have chosen and go through the following exercise:

1. Close your eyes and put yourself into the work of art.
2. Imagine embodying the image.
3. What does it feel like to be inside this frame?
4. How does whatever is depicted in the image see or experience the world?
5. What lens is the artist or the creator of this work of art peering through?

Jot down a few adjectives that describe the lenses each work of art evokes for you.

Example: Lens brainstorm of Picasso's *Girl in the Mirror*—personal, evocative, confusing, colorful, vulnerable.

Choose one lens per image and write them here:

1. *Girl in the Mirror*: colorful

2. *Portrait of Michelle Obama*: lit-from-within (this is a phrase I got from a coaching client who did this exercise and chose this painting)

3. *Autumn Rhythm*: chaos

Now, take each of those lenses and return to your current situation. Look through each of the lenses you parsed out from different works of art.

Ask yourself, what would it be like to look at my current situation through the lens of each one?

Example:

Current Situation: I am editing my book

Current Lens: overwhelming

Other lenses to try:

Examples:

Colorful: Picasso sees brilliant color and pattern in places you would not expect. If I viewed the editorial process as an opportunity to bring out the colors in my work, things I may not have seen or read at first glance, it starts to feel exciting and creative instead of overwhelming.

Lit-from-within: Amy Sherald makes Michelle Obama shimmer with confidence and an inner light. The editorial process through the lens of lit-from-within feels hopeful. It allows me to erase large swaths of writing with the confidence that everything I need is here; it is just a matter of letting it shine through.

Chaotic: Pollock's image feels powerful and active, almost screaming from the canvas. Chaos is depicted beautifully here, but organizing the squiggly lines seems impossible. Trying on the lens of "chaotic" as I view my editorial process gives me some perspective. Like Pollock's painting has a frame, my current situation is containable. There are not an infinite number of pages or words.

Name your lenses in your journal and explore how they help shift your perspective.

Lens 1:

Lens 2:

Lens 3:

What have you learned in this étude?

What lens would you like to choose today? Can you give it a name?

CODA ⊕

According to Nasa's website,

> To apply to be an astronaut, you must meet the following qualifications:

- Be a U.S. citizen.

- Possess a master's degree in a STEM field, including engineering, biological science, physical science, computer science, or mathematics, from an accredited institution.

- Have at least two years of related professional experience obtained after degree completion or at least 1,000 hours pilot-in-command time on jet aircraft.

- Be able to pass the NASA long-duration flight astronaut physical.

- Candidates must also have skills in leadership, teamwork, and communications.

In 2016, they had 18,300 applications. A "small group of the most highly qualified" are invited to interview, and a handful of those are selected. Of the astronauts selected, only a certain number will go to space. A total of 550 people in history have been to space; two-thirds of those are Americans.

Being an artist is not like being an astronaut. Extended training is available if you'd like to learn the specifics of a craft, but you were an artist before you considered art school or music conservatory. Don't fall into the trap of thinking someone needs to give you permission to make stuff you care about or follow your dreams; creativity is as basic as breathing. It isn't for just the special, talented, elite, and trainable. It is as necessary and satisfying as a delicious meal is when you are hungry. Being an artist is our human right, privilege, and calling. How would your life look different through that lens?

Being an artist is not like being an astronaut.

Five True Things (don't forget to add yours):

1. "Comparison is the thief of joy" (Theodore Roosevelt).

2. Being an artist is not like being an astronaut.

3. Someone will always be better, but there will never be another me.

4. Creativity is tapas, not pie.

5. *I can view my challenges through different lenses to help me get unstuck.*

PART THREE

Recapitulation
The Theme Returns

re·ca·pit·u·la·tion (noun)

1. An act or instance of summarizing and restating the main points of something.

2. The repetition of an evolutionary or other process during development or growth.

3. A part of a movement (especially one in sonata form) in which themes from the exposition are restated.

How I picture it: We are all nesting dolls, carrying the earlier iterations of ourselves inside. We carry the past inside us. Inside forty-something me is the woman I was in my thirties, the woman I was in my twenties, the teenager I was, the child I was. We take ourselves—all of our selves—wherever we go. It is a kind of reincarnation without death; all these different lives we get to live in this one body, as ourselves.

—Maggie Smith, *You Could Make This Place Beautiful*

Introduction to Part III
Coming Home to Yourself

Joy is sensing the world's rightness. It is letting the theme lead you home after the long episodic development.

As you sit back in your chair and take a breath, you're aware that there are more pages on the left side of the spine than on the right.

The Exposition explored the basic internal sense of work we begin within ourselves, how we find a creative rhythm of devotion, learn to care for our bodies, and change slowly with intentionality. The Development took these tools for a dance through the world, exploring the obstacles we may encounter there. And part III, the Recapitulation, returns us to our internal work, now deeper and more resonant, with a new awareness of all the "selves" we each contain within us, as Maggie Smith reflects.

The chapters in the final part explore how creativity can be a spiritual practice. Beyond being a career path, a vocation, or a passion, within the seeds of creativity lies an opportunity for deep spiritual connection and, ultimately, healing. When we seek answers to questions about the nature of inspiration, courage, and our innate worthiness, we begin to see that sustainable joy is found when we harmonize what is within and beyond us to craft a sustainable artistic practice that feeds our soul.

ELEVEN

Ode to Courage
The Momentum Fear Provides

Act II, Coda, Fouette, from *Swan Lake*, Op. 20,
by Pyotr Ilyich Tchaikovsky

If not now, when?

—Rabbi Hillel, *The Talmud*

EMMIE

I didn't know until I lived with a ballerina how gnarly their feet look up close. At my arts boarding school, our suitemate, Emmie, would grace us with her presence a couple of evenings per week as she sewed new pointe shoes or tended to her blisters. Emmie had confidence that only dancing since you were a fetus could bring. Her body had been shaped by fifteen years of athleticism and intense training, boarding school during the school year, and the American Ballet Theater training program every summer.

One night, the conversation turned to the gossip in the dance world, the fact that a new principal ballerina, all the rage on the world's stage, was under scrutiny for only completing twelve of the thirty-two fouetté turns required when dancing the role of Odile in *Swan Lake*.

"How does one even begin to do that, spin that many times?" I asked Emmie.

"Well, just like you do every other sequence. You dance Acts I and II. You do the variation. You wait for your music and do thirty-two spins on the same leg."

"Oh, that simple, huh?"

When we run from fear, we miss momentum.

THE DAY I GOT THE CALL

It was an average December night in New York City. I was practicing at a friend's apartment in the mid-thirties on the far east side of the island. A few days before Christmas, the semester had ended, and I was practicing some music for a Christmas eve gig when I heard my phone ping, a message from my oboe teacher at Juilliard.

"The third oboist in the orchestra for the *Girl of the Golden West* tonight at the Metropolitan Opera has been in a car accident on the way to the hall. She's fine but won't make it here in time. Could you step in?"

I looked at the clock. It was 7:23 p.m. The downbeat was at 8:00 p.m. I had thirty-seven minutes to find black clothing (which I luckily had on), grab my instrument (which was in my hand), and get across town to Lincoln Center.

This was that moment they always talk about, I thought to myself. *That moment when the call comes in, and it's your chance. Was I ready?* I had no time to answer that. I typed, "I'm on my way," and sent it. Her next text described where I was to meet the personnel manager for the orchestra at the stage door, explaining that I would be escorted to my seat in the pit. She also said, "This live broadcast will be on Sirius XM radio tonight." Gulp.

I decided to take the subway, even though it was not the most direct route. (By the way, if you ever find yourself in a hurry in New York City, the subway is always faster, ask a cab driver. Trust me, you'll thank me later.) I walked/ran to Grand Central Station while breathlessly calling my parents to tell them to turn on the radio. I grabbed the S train to Times Square, switched to the 1, and exited at Lincoln Center at 65th Street and Broadway.

By 7:52 p.m., I was in the pit. I felt the eyes of everyone in the wind section as I found my way to the third oboe chair. The lights blinked, alerting the audience to take their seats. The principal bassoonist, seated behind me, leaned forward, tapped me on the shoulder, and said, "Hey . . . you can definitely hear the third oboe part at letter M in Act II."

I frantically flipped to through my music, but my teacher to the left of me said, "Act I is first. Use the intermission to look through Act II. Watch the key signatures. You never play alone, so you're in the wrong place if we aren't with you."

And then came the downbeat.

Two and a half hours of Puccini later, I had made my Met Opera debut.

THE THREE W'S OF COURAGE

As scary and risky as it was, on the surface sight-reading an opera with one of the world's best orchestras live on the radio did take immense courage. But if I'm honest, sometimes being an oboist at all—being an *artist* at all—feels like a courageous act in and of itself.

Coaching clients often think courage is this Herculean force they either have or don't.

When I got that call that night, the call I thought would change everything—it didn't change much beyond my plans for that evening and a few other nights when I got to return and sub again, by the way—I realized the need for courage doesn't stop or start when the "big break" comes. The artist's life takes courage like playing the oboe takes air. Better still, I believe courage is something we can cultivate for more creative joy.

The artist's life takes courage like playing the oboe takes air.

You are already much more courageous than you even know. Picking up this book and reading this far is courageous; it shows that you believe your inner artist is someone to be invested in. Being an artist in the world means believing in something that you cannot yet see. The blank canvas and oils can become a painting, the scale becomes music, only in the hands of the hopeful and courageous artist.

So, why can't we face the uncertainty and paralyzing fear that undoubtedly appears when we answer the calls that come in? How do we continue saying yes to all the creative life offers without self-sabotage?

How do we develop more courage?

NO. 1: NAME YOUR "WHY" (FOR NOW)

Simon Sinek's book, *Start with Why*, took the world by storm in 2009, helping companies and individuals name the motivation behind their life or product. Rick Warren's international bestseller, *A Purpose Driven Life* (2002), was a similar phenomenon. If you came of age at a certain time, you might have been inundated with talk about what you were born to do, achieve, or creatively offer to the world, all while the sands of the hourglass drift away forever, never to be returned to you.

If that isn't anxiety-inducing, I'm not sure what is.

In a conversation with Kate Bowler, Elizabeth Gilbert calls this "purpose anxiety." Feeling straight-jacketed by your life's purpose is never the goal. And yet, I didn't think twice about packing up my oboe and heading across town that night, even though I was scared, because that was why I was in NYC in the first place. I had come there to study the oboe, to become an oboist, and so, of course, I would say yes when someone offered me a chance to do that, even though it was very scary. The lessons from early chapters have helped us stay connected to our inner artist-child, so when our life speaks, we hear it.

There is a way to name your "Why" that gives you strength and courage instead of anxiety. When we name and claim the purpose or mission behind our creative practice, considering our season of life, courage becomes a force that catapults us toward the dream.

We have learned that when fear shows up, it can cause the negative inner voices of anxiety to chatter. It is easy to talk yourself out of taking scary steps forward if you are listening to those voices, but when you see them as trying to protect you as you take a necessary risk, the voices can be confirmation that you are on the right path. At the end of the chapter, we will name the "Why (for Now)." You will reflect and state your creative mission in your current life season—staying deeply connected to your "Why" (for now or forever) is the first step to cultivating courage.

NO. 2: DO THE WORK

The second W of courage is work—letting your creative devotion routine and your dedication to it be the net that catches you when you leap forward. We stay connected to our values to help us make decisions, but once we decide who and what we want to be, we commit to taking small steps every day to get there. In chapter 3, we discussed devotion instead of discipline: how showing up at the desk or the instrument with that mindset keeps you from getting burnt out, injured, or dis*couraged*. (Interesting word in this context, no?)

There will be days when you feel like it isn't worth it or it's too hard; keep doing the work anyway. It fills the courage bank account you will desperately need to pull from later when you wonder if you're ready. The work you do out of devotion each morning may not be for today or the next day. It may be years from now when you get the call, start the business, or do the scary thing that feels like taking a leap of faith; the work you did is the net that will catch you.

The process—not the product—helps us build courage. When the call doesn't come or the work isn't recognized, we keep going. The process—not the product—helps us build courage. The work also gives you wisdom and strength you cannot see yet. It helps you know when to step out into the arena (or the pit, in my case). Trusting the process means letting your training and practice be the gift you give yourself in the face of the immensely risky thing you are about to do creatively.

NO. 3: WHIRL

When I saw Emmie cast as Odile on the poster outside of the theater that day in New York, I thought back to what she'd said all those years ago. I wondered if she believed there was more to it now than just "wait for the music, start spinning." Lots of us have blind confidence and audacity when we are young, but I believe there was something true in what Emmie was saying, too.

If you've ever watched a ballerina, you've seen Newton's Law of Motion in action, the law that says an object in motion tends to stay in motion unless acted upon by an unbalanced force. The spinning dancer has strength, poise, and balance but also has something underrated: momentum. Fear provides a certain energy that, when combined with work and connection to our "why," can propel us into that first spin and then the next and then the next. And the feat of thirty-two spins unfolds one at a time, thank God.

We don't need the courage to do thirty-two, we need enough courage to do one and then one more. Do not worry about Act II; be inside the spin you're in. Trust that momentum will take you right back around for another. Don't let the fear unbalance you. Make it work for you; believe your knobby feet will hold you upright.

For those of us who do not have a teacher beside us or a conductor before us giving our musical cue, how do we know when? When to take the call? Or the audition? To submit the work? To start to spin?

The answer is now—because, as the ancient wisdom goes—when else? If not you, then who? If you are waiting for confidence before you act, you may be waiting forever. And when failure no longer has the power to destroy your identity, like we learned in chapter 8, fear loses its paralyzing power. Instead, it gives us the momentum to whirl.

SELF-COACHING QUESTIONS

1. What would you do if you were not afraid of failing?

2. Look at your creative routine: how is it working for you now? Revisit chapter 3 for ideas about deepening your creative devotion.

3. What do the negative inner voices say to you when you step beyond your comfort zone?

4. Are your thoughts generally encouraging or discouraging you? How would your positive inner voices answer the negative outbursts? Write a short letter to your negative inner voices in your journal.

5. Who in your life seems to have a lot of creative courage? Interview them like I did Emmie. How do they do hard things?

ÉTUDE: YOUR "WHY (FOR NOW)"

Review the études in chapters 4, 5, and 6 and read your responses. By now, you should have a fairly good idea of what matters to you and a list of your dreams and goals you have on deck.

Naming your "Why (for Now)" at this stage in personal development can be powerful because you are already so connected with internal motivators.

Purpose anxiety can make us feel pressure to make every hard moment, dead-end job, lame gig, or bad day worse because it all has to serve some cosmic purpose. Sometimes things happen. Sometimes we do work adjacent to our purpose for decades, and that's ok. Sometimes we accidentally discover that what we want is a hobby instead of a new creative career.

Naming your purpose is powerful in helping you realize your motivation. Creativity coach Eric Maisel has you name your life purpose statement in his popular book *Coaching the Artist Within*. It can give you energy and help you get clear when making decisions. But to keep it from causing you undue purpose anxiety, I pair it with Kendra Adachi's advice to "Learn to live in your season." You are also not the person you were ten years ago or even three months ago in some areas of your life. Naming the season of life first and then the "Why" of this particular now is a powerful way to get the most out of Simon Sinek's idea without having to feel the pressure of naming THE thing that gives your life meaning and direction for all time and eternity.

Follow the prompts to name the Why (for Now).

Describe the current season of your life:

What are your biggest goals in this season?

What do you need most right now?

What natural barriers in life are framing this season (i.e., graduation day, kids starting school, residency ending)?

What is possible in this season? What is not?

Who is walking alongside you on the hard days?

Season title:

Examples: Raising little ones or finishing undergrad
Discovering your why in the season you are in:

What makes you feel most alive lately?

What is uniquely yours to do in this moment of your life?

Where do the world's needs meet your gifts?

What do your friends/colleagues/random strangers say they love most about you? (If you aren't sure, Simon Sinek says to ask them and then ask them again until you get the answer that resonates.)

Name your Why (for Now): Why do you do what you do in this season? What is your purpose now?

Your Why (for Now):

CODA ⊕

The finals of the 2022 FIFA World Cup in Qatar broke a record for the number of games decided via penalty shootout in a World Cup tournament ever: and that number is five. (I suppose even I can be a sportsperson when there is a metaphor involved.)

Five different games went to penalty kicks because the score was tied even after extra time. Penalty shootouts mean each team goes to the goal and takes a turn shooting, the best out of five wins.

Watching the teams huddle around the goal, which suddenly looks like cavernous jaws threatening to swallow the poor goalie whole, everyone's eyes are on that player, who literally has a split second to decide. Jump left or jump right.

Which way will you jump?

We make the best call we can with the information we have at the time. And sometimes a ball gets by us. We cannot be all things to all people, we cannot always win. Being a courageous, creative person means making the best decision you can, staying connected to your "Why," and doing the work. Believing the game is designed to be won doesn't guarantee that we will always go right when the ball does. But I don't know about you; even when I lose, I know *But I don't know about you; even when I lose, I know I would much rather be guarding the goal, playing that game, than standing on the sidelines.* I would much rather be guarding the goal, playing that game, than standing on the sidelines.

You'll see in the next two chapters that courage is a key component in feeling worthy and cultivating joy in your creative life. Brené Brown says, "Courage starts with showing up and letting ourselves be seen."

You can take the subway or the cab to Lincoln Center. Which way will you go? Trust yourself enough to know that whatever direction you choose, the courage to jump, to show up at all, is what counts. Being on the field, being willing to risk it all in the name of what matters most to you, in service to the person you are becoming—that's a goal no one can take away from you, regardless of the final score of the game.

Five True Things (don't forget to add yours):

1. In the face of negative inner voices or imposter syndrome thoughts, I step forward anyway.

2. Living well in the season you're in helps with purpose anxiety.

3. When I leap, the work catches me.

4. Fear can be repurposed and redirected.

5.

TWELVE

Ode to Self-Forgiveness

Loving Yourself When You Don't Love Your Art

"Adagio," from *Cello Quintet in C*, by Franz Schubert

Music, we like to say, is about time. Whereas a Beethoven can seem to enlist time in a glorious ride to the future, Schubert makes us feel its irrevocable passing. We hear the sound of memory, the sound of mortality—and it is beautiful.

—Scott Burnham, "Schubert and the Sound of Memory"

RYAN

The foster-care system had made Ryan a great storyteller. At least there was that. When I met him, he had recently finished the manuscript of his first book, a memoir, all about his early life, before his bipolar mother, a poet, had died. I asked him the first question I always ask my clients when they finish a project: "How are you celebrating?" Ryan was initially reluctant.

Eventually, he decided to take a trip alone to a cabin near a lake, and when he got there, he performed the ritual we had discussed in the coaching session before. Light a candle, stand it up with melted wax in a biodegradable boat, say a prayer, and release it across the lake. As it floated precariously toward the dam on the other side, he prayed that his book proposal would find its way into the hands of the right person.

When he returned from the trip, a different kind of work began. He started the query process. Emailing agents and publishers with his pitch, he told them (in two hundred words or less) why they should take him on as a writer and why his book mattered. That was one year ago. He came back to coaching tired and beaten down.

"It's death by a million cuts," he said. "Most of the time, I hear nothing. Sometimes, mercifully they respond and say they pass, but I get more silence when I ask for a reason. One even asked me to change the whole project into a work of fiction. Everyone keeps saying not to take it personally, but how could I not? This is literally the story of my life."

Learning to stop waiting on the world to love you, to start loving yourself, that is the work of the artist. And we do that by practicing radical self-forgiveness.

Learning to stop waiting on the world to love you, to start loving yourself, that is the work of the artist. And we do that by practicing radical self-forgiveness.

THE SOUND IN MY HEAD

I heard a famous oboist say publicly once that playing the oboe is like bungee jumping.

In my creative recovery groups, we do an exercise where we name the metaphor of our creative impulse that resonates most. (I will invite you to try this in chapter 14's études.) I've heard it described as a simmering sauce to sprouting seedlings or wearing a giant horse head while on roller skates. Most people's metaphors express vulnerability or the need for patience, sometimes absurdity and humor; they all feel true. And as much as I hate to admit it, the bungee jumping one also tracks.

There is this oboe sound I have in my head. It's full and rich and varied, like an incandescent rock that takes on different shades of light as you tilt it this way and that. I dream of my oboe sounding a certain way and that it will feel as easy as inhaling. And I soak the reeds, put the instrument together, and wait there on the side of the bungee platform, praying the hours of practice and reed-making will catch me. I sit in the orchestra, counting the measures until I enter with an exposed solo after not playing a note for the last fifteen minutes of the strings' interlude. Two more measures. The blood rushes to my head, and that exhilarating feeling of leaping takes over. I enter on time.

Some days, it feels easy; other days it feels like getting jerked around by inanimate objects. Even when it feels great, I hear a recording and realize the sound in my head was a pipe dream. We have faith that the work we do will catch us when we jump. We dare to step off the platform.

It was the novelist Ann Patchett who reminded me that, after we jump, what we really need is self-forgiveness. In her essay, "The Getaway Car," she explores her own simile for writing a novel; it is like seeing a butterfly flying around her head. She sits with the idea as it flutters about, and, for a long time, she simply admires it, lets the whole thing come to her perfectly in her head. Eventually, she knows she must start trying to put this story that's been, up to this point, in her head, on paper. She compares that process to grabbing that butterfly out of the air and pinning it down. That process inevitably kills the insect, which is never as beautiful as when she first imagined it.

She writes,

Forgiveness. The ability to forgive oneself . . . it is the key to making art and very possibly the key to finding any semblance of happiness in life. Every time I have set out to translate the book that exists in such brilliant detail on the big screen of my limbic system onto a piece of paper, I grieve for my own lack of talent and intelligence. Every. Single. Time. Were I smarter, more gifted, I could pin down a closer facsimile of the wonders I see. I believe, more than anything, that this grief of constantly having to face down our own inadequacies is what keeps people from being writers. Forgiveness, therefore, is key. I can't write the book I want to write, but I can and will write the book I am capable of writing. Again and again, throughout the course of my life, I will forgive myself.

I cannot replicate the sound I have in my head, and self-forgiveness is the only way to love myself in the midst of this pursuit.

SOUNDS OF MEMORY AND MORTALITY

A few years into my creative recovery journey, after I left New York, I did feel better. I was playing chamber music in Chicago, making money doing a thing I loved, albeit not much. I felt motivated and stable most days, but then something would happen where I'd feel a familiar bitterness rise.

One day during that time, I was lying on the floor of my then friend, now husband's, apartment. A massive storm was rolling in, and we were both looking out the one window at the sky. It was one of those warm summer evenings where one minute it was bright and sunny, and next thing you know, thick black clouds covered the whole day, not unlike the unpredictable patterns of my own personality at that time. Edwin loved storms. We camped out under the window, he played music, and we watched nature bring the rain.

After a small lull in conversation, he asked me a seemingly benign question: "What is your favorite piece of classical music?" As a Latin jazz percussionist, he didn't know much about the oboe or the classical world (blissfully, I remember thinking) and he was curious to learn about his new friend and her music. I always dreaded these questions from him and everyone, especially at that stage of my creative recovery. There was still a wound there. But I couldn't explain that to him then; we had just met.

Much to my surprise (maybe it was the storm or the new relationship), I told him that one of my favorite pieces of classical music was the second movement of the Schubert *Cello Quintet*, a piece I'd written a set of papers about during my doctorate, a piece I swore never to listen to again after I left the halls of Juilliard.

He pulled a recording up, and, as it played, I gave him a play-by-play of what Schubert was doing in this, one of his final works. I explained to him what I heard in it: a composer struggling with his identity and his mortality. His time on Earth was slipping away, and he knew it. In my opinion, the *Cello Quintet* was his best piece, yet the composer never got to hear it performed live in his lifetime.

Suddenly, things I had sworn to forget poured out of me. The way that the opening melody doesn't sound like a melody, like it's missing something. How the middle section is stormy and unsettling with this almost terrifying rumbling in the second cello. When the opening melody returns, Schubert leaves some of the terror from the second section in, which composers never do. In the recapitulation, the themes were supposed to return to how they were originally presented, but Schubert didn't do that. He left the rumbles in the recap and with it he left "memory and mortality," as Scott Burnham wrote. I believed this was a message from the composer on his deathbed. Like he was saying, "No one is the same after the experience of this life. There are rumbles that leave melodies changed forever. But watch me make something beautiful out of it anyway."

These were things I hadn't thought of in years.

With them came shame, from feeling like the degree was a waste of time, that I hadn't been as successful as I'd dreamt I'd be. There was pain and guilt about all the ways that I was to blame for how I let myself be pushed to the brink of exhaustion and burnout. The sound in my head was not the sound of my instrument. The life that I was leading was not one I had envisioned. The butterfly I'd pinned down looked nothing like it did in my mind. And it was all my fault.

As Edwin and I lay there listening, as I heard the strings swell, my heart suddenly broke open like a cloud of water. Music *did* still move me. As much pain as I had experienced over the years, this fact was simply part of me; it was a calling, after all, despite all the ways I thought I had failed at it. I saw then some of the ways life and all its rumbles had changed *me*.

Through that music, I heard Schubert again, "To love, you must forgive yourself, like I never could."

It was then, lying on a floor with a friend, watching a storm, listening to a composer who died penniless and unrecognized, that my theme was returned to me. And it resonated differently this time—with self-compassion and grace.

Love and forgiveness are inextricably linked. Through forgiveness, we choose to love the imperfectly whole artists we are. That's why I believe this was so central to Ann Patchett's sustainable writing life. Love without forgiveness is only skin deep.

> *Love and forgiveness are inextricably linked. Through forgiveness, we choose to love the imperfectly whole artists we are.*

The space between who we dream of being as artists and who we end up being, between what we see in our mind's eye and what we actually create—in order to love ourselves, we must forgive ourselves for that gap. The answer is not lowering our standards. Anyone who has seen those butterflies knows that that is impossible. Forgive yourself for your shortcomings, for all the ways it is not perfect, for falling short of all you'd dreamed you'd do. Forgive yourself for mistakes you have made, big and small. Never think for a moment that you are a mistake.

If Ann Patchett stopped trying to pin down the butterflies because of her perceived lack of ability, the world would be less beautiful for it. Loving yourself well—finding sustainability as a creator—means heaping constant self-forgiveness on your head.

What if you can't forgive yourself? What if you self-sabotaged so bad you can't come back from it? Or what if, like Ryan, you needed that memoir, that story of your life, to be published so you could believe that your life wasn't a waste, that all your pain and suffering had been turned into something beautiful? I can hear Ryan saying, "How could I forgive myself for failing to tell that story compellingly? My inner artist-child trusted me to get it down on paper, but I failed. It's unforgivable."

I would ask, to that I *did* ask, "What is there calling out for forgiveness, Ryan?"

He choked up. "Since my mother was too mentally ill to raise me, since I was too old to find a forever home in the system, I guess I keep looking to art to justify myself, my existence, my pain. I've just transferred that longing for a family onto some publisher." "That's too much pressure for a book," he said after a beat.

That's when Ryan had the idea of sharing his manuscript with other adults formerly in foster care. He connected with a small group of men and women who had grown up in the system; they formed a book club. They absolutely loved his story; they held space for it with great care. He found some of his "ones." He is still hoping to get the book traditionally published, but that connection with others helped him offer forgiveness to his writer self; it helped him let go of the outcome a little, offer grace, and let love rush in.

Playing the oboe is much safer than bungee jumping, but only if I am compassionate and offer forgiveness when the sound in my head does not come close to the one on the recording. Whatever your creative impulse metaphor, we struggle with perfectionism and shame until we become people of grace.

I learned from Brené Brown in an interview with Harriet Lerner to resist the temptation to follow an apology with "It's okay," because sometimes it isn't okay. Say "I forgive you" instead. Saying to yourself, "I forgive you for not winning that audition. I forgive you for failing to follow up with that lead. I forgive you for not being perfect or even good sometimes," it doesn't mean you are ok with it. Forgiveness doesn't have to mean that you have healed or have forgotten. It just means you'll no longer let the pain caused by the wrong continue turning into bitterness and hatred, continue stealing your joy.

Loving and forgiving yourself takes practice and hard work, just like loving a spouse, friend, or family member. But your behavior, performance, and art's reception are not tools to measure your worthiness. We will explore this more next.

The work of the artist is a work of forgiveness. Let this self-compassion soften you, especially when you feel you have failed.

> *The work of the artist is a work of forgiveness.*

SELF-COACHING QUESTIONS

1. What is hardest about self-forgiveness for you? Anger? Pride?

2. Which parts of your creative practice feel most personal to you?

3. How are love and forgiveness connected in your life experience?

4. What decisions are ahead that will require courage and compassion? How will you know when it is time to leap?

5. Who in your life knows about your creative failures or U-turns? Whom do you trust enough to share them with?

ÉTUDE: SELF-FORGIVENESS LIST

Make two columns in your journal. In column 2 to the right side of the paper, write a list of all the painful things that sting in your creative life.

Not winning that audition

Failing to follow up with that person about that opportunity

Not being able to please this or that person

And then in column 1, to the left of that, write:

I forgive you for . . . by each one

Read them out loud to yourself. If they do not seem true today, keep coming back to them until they do. And remember, saying I forgive you is different than saying, "It's okay." Sometimes it isn't okay. After you finish the exercise, do something kind and loving for yourself, like call a friend or buy a favorite beverage.

CODA ⊕

A horse's eye is one of the largest eyes of all land mammals. For context, the human range of vision is 150 degrees, whereas horses see 350 degrees around their bodies. They can almost see all the way around, due to their eyes' size and their lateral placement on the horses' long slender heads. But those who train and ride likely know that bigger eyes do not always mean greater vision. For example, when a horse goes to jump, there is a moment when the object below them disappears completely from their field of sight. It can be hard for horses to see what is right below them. They react by getting skittish. They back up, and lift their front legs as they gallop toward a hurdle. When they can't see, they turn back at the last minute and circle the field a few more times before attempting the jump again. They want to keep the obstacle they're jumping over in their field of sight, and when it disappears, they get nervous and scared, understandably.

Is your own limited field of vision making you skittish? There's only so much you can see ahead of you, right? And sometimes, with the hurdle you're attempting to clear, regardless of how big, strong, and prepared you feel, there's a moment where you must leap even though you can't see what is right there.

Creativity is a leap of faith. It requires of us a fierce courage and trust, and self-love and forgiveness are either side of the bridle of a joyful creative ride.

> *Creativity is a leap of faith. It requires of us a fierce courage and trust, and self-love and forgiveness are either side of the bridle of a joyful creative ride.*

It's tempting to keep circling; it's normal to want always to keep that hurdle in your line of sight, to want control and awareness because the "what if's" are scary. What if you fall? What if you get hurt? What if you clear that one, and they raise the next one higher? What if . . .? But regardless of the height of the fences to clear, horses, like artists, are capable of beautiful, powerful, and graceful leaps of faith.

And here's the thing: on top of many great horses is a great rider at the reins. So, we aren't alone when we leap. First, because we have each other, and we also have our own inner jockey. It's not some wild animal, but another set of eyes, our inner artist—and we can trust that that jockey knows what to do. The jockey, with equal amounts of love and forgiveness at the ready, knows that there is life after every leap, regardless of how many times we circle or how many fences we've clipped in the past.

An artist's eye can see many things the average human eye cannot, and isn't that a gift? But we mustn't let the places where our vision fails us make us skittish; we can't let it stop us from jumping. No matter what disappointing, heart-wrenching creative U-turns you've taken in your life, no matter how beautiful your butter-flies are, or how much you've had to forgive, it's not too late to circle back and love again.

Five True Things (don't forget to add yours):

1. "The ability to forgive oneself . . . it is the key to making art and very possibly the key to finding any semblance of happiness in life" (Ann Patchett).

2. A brave, creative life can leave a mark.

3. No matter how many fences I've clipped in the past, there is life after every leap.

4. Love without forgiveness is only skin deep.

5.

THIRTEEN

Ode to Worthiness
Your Work Is Not Your Worth

Après un Rêve (1878), by Gabriel Fauré

When you get to a place where you understand that love and belonging, your worthiness, is a birthright and not something you have to earn, anything is possible.
—Brené Brown, "Being Vulnerable About Vulnerability"

VIVIAN

"I got my dream job," she said, distraught.

Last I'd heard from Vivian, she had been working part-time for a symphony orchestra, designing educational shows for kids using hip-hop to teach the basic elements of music. Her passion for using the arts to serve and her devotion to the orchestra's mission to be more community-focused brought the orchestra multiple large grants. They were ready to fund a full-time program and wanted Vivian to run it.

So, on the one hand, she was thrilled. This was beyond her wildest imagination—the orchestra director and outside funders validated a program she'd started. But, as her voice on the other line revealed, Vivian was plagued by anxiety. The orchestra had asked for her "number," how much she wanted to make when she became full-time.

"That's when the waking in the night started," she said. "I'd wake up sweating from a dream, but not about anything I could remember. I keep hearing these voices saying, 'Who do you think you are, asking for that salary? You didn't even go to college! You aren't worth that!'"

When faced with goodness, the greatest challenge can be believing we are worthy.

HOW TO SATISFY YOUR EGO

Running from my own imposter syndrome, I washed up on the shores of Lake Michigan and found myself in a church in downtown Chicago. One of my three part-time jobs that paid my rent was coordinating music lessons for children and seniors in this church. One sunny Saturday, I met a man who seemed to come from a completely different world; his clergy collar seemed at odds with his long jet-black hair, which he wore tightly in a ponytail. I asked him to swipe me a plate of food from the men's breakfast in the fellowship hall—our friendship was sealed.

After a few weeks of knowing Edwin, he came right out and asked me something he'd been wondering since day one. "Why is it when you tell me about someone in your life, the first fact you say about them besides their name is where they went to school?" He paused. "Ian Eastman. Sara Curtis. It must be important, where someone studied?"

I don't remember what I said at that moment. I think I laughed or attempted to blow it off. Maybe I got defensive. He didn't seem like he was trying to be argumentative, just genuinely curious and slightly confused. I cringe when I think about it now. Being unfamiliar with the names of music schools, he had thought Eastman or Curtis were these friends' last names.

I know now from my creative recovery work that I'm not the only one inclined to do such things. We attempt to satisfy our ego with thoughts of superiority when we fail or flop in a big way: *Well, at least I . . . [name your largest accomplishment that makes you feel better than someone else here].* When I got into Juilliard, an acquaintance, a graduate of that institution himself, said, "The best part of going to Juilliard is that you get to say you went to Juilliard." I think at the time I snickered. But it is not funny now. Once Edwin pointed it out, I realized I was making my resumé mean something about myself, something I desperately needed to be true. It was what made me feel worthy.

Juilliard, winning a big job, and being a *New York Times* best seller are not bad things in and of themselves. That is, until they become ultimate. Celebrating success is an important and joyful act. Yet when our achievements become our whole identity, we feel good about ourselves at someone else's expense and dangerously tie our worthiness to our performance.

What happens when we don't perform well? Or when the second book flops, or we don't get into Juilliard (like 94% of the people who apply, by the way)? When we confuse our work with our worthiness, our failure becomes despair.

If you wonder if this is only a classical music or a Juilliard thing, as a creativity coach, I have seen that every discipline has its own way of satisfying the ego. Just ask yourself who you envy. What school did they attend? What awards have they won? What did they do that you did not?

Fill in these sentences with the first thing that comes to mind.

My greatest accomplishment is _my children (whole story_.
I know I am welcome at the creative table because of my _talent_.
I don't belong at the creative table because I haven't _sold enough paintings_.
If only I had _a gallery_, then I would know I had made it.
If only I had not screwed up _my life_, then I'd be on track.
Real artists are the ones who _make a living with their work_.

Are you placing your value and sense of worthiness (or lack thereof) in whatever words are in those blanks? Underneath my superiority was insecurity, underneath that, the fear of failure.

A DEEPER WORTHINESS

Imposter syndrome comes up with nearly all my coaching clients. Studies show that many of us, regardless of gender, age, experience level, or ethnic group, have doubts about our abilities.

I've gotten used to these inner antics of my monkey mind and become friends with them. I learned in my coaching training that these voices show up when we step out of our comfort zone when we are trying something new. They don't mean we aren't good enough; it's just a brain trying to keep us safe. When the voices appear, it doesn't mean we are on the wrong track; it means we are growing.

When I read Brené Brown's *The Gifts of Imperfection*, I felt like the world's weight was lifted from my shoulders. Learning that vulnerability is the antidote to perfectionism, that we free ourselves from shame by talking about it, I knew that being well meant doing things that were often counterintuitive to the shame-based cultures in so many arts institutions. And amazingly, in my creative recovery work, I learned that worthiness, too, is something we can learn and practice.

In Brown's research, courage, compassion, and connection are the three key values that help us practice worthiness. Practicing, not perfecting it. She says, "We become more courageous by doing courageous acts, we invite compassion into our lives when we act compassionately towards ourselves and others, and we feel connected in our lives when we reach out and connect."

Connection is the high note of the worthiness chord we've built in the last three chapters. That question from my nonmusician friend helped me see, maybe for the first time, that I had some major work to do around self-worth.

FIND A FRIEND TO TELL YOU THE TRUTH

When Vivian told me she felt unworthy of that job and its salary because she hadn't gone to college, I knew I had to tell her what I'd learned from that friendship, from creative recovery. I started with my resumé not to satisfy my ego but to douse the flame of insecurities with truth.

"Vivian, I went to twelve years of college. I have an Ivy League degree. I was a Fulbright Scholar and have a music doctorate from school with a 6.7 percent acceptance rate. None of that made me feel worthy. You can't outrun the 'if only.' There will always be someone more talented, more celebrated, and more successful than you. You can't win your way to worthiness; you can't outrun the shame by performance or achievement. It doesn't work like that. Trust me, I've tried."

Vivian did her research, asked for a salary that she believed was fair, and they said yes. Sometimes, when we are faced with our own insecurities, we need to find a friend to tell us something true.

Sometimes, when we are faced with our own insecurities, we need to find a friend to tell us something true.

If we are going to take Brené Brown at her word, which, of course, we should—then first, courage: flip back to chapter 12 and remember your Why (for Now), show up at the desk or to the studio with devotion, and let fear give you momentum to move forward. Then rush in with compassion for all the ways you may believe you have failed. Be about the work of self-forgiveness, as we learned in chapter 13.

As for connection, perhaps you have noticed by now that there is always a self-coaching question at the end of each chapter that requires you to look around and realize you are not alone. Who in your life can you call when you're feeling shame? Who can tell you the truth about your belovedness? What communities do you belong to? Pick up the phone when the hungry lion of ego, fueled by anxiety and shame, makes you wonder what you're worth. I hope I was able to offer Vivian compassion and connection, but even more than that, I hope I inspired her to offer that to herself and those she serves through the power of music.

We will return to the "if only" statements at the end of the chapter, restating them using a courageous and compassionate rephrase, but for now, know that your worthiness is inborn.

It is as central to your existence as your DNA, a quality you already hold.

It is unconditional and unwavering.

Nothing you can do puts your worthiness in jeopardy.

The fact that you are alive makes you worthy.

When you pitch an idea, your value, merit, or innate goodness are not in play.

Practicing worthiness is an act of creative recovery because your creative work will always come from a place of fear until you know, regardless of how you are received, that your life has value; that is not something you could ever earn or lose.

Practicing worthiness is an act of creative recovery because your creative work will always come from a place of fear until you know, regardless of how you are received, that your life has value; that is not something you could ever earn or lose.

It is something you already are.

It is something you already are.

As Brené Brown reminds us, when we believe that, anything is possible.

As you can tell from my reciting people's college degrees in lieu of their names, in the classical music world, people put much emphasis on where and with whom they studied. Once Edwin pointed out that I was doing that, I made it a goal to ask better questions of people, to see them for more than their resumé, to see myself for more, too. This way of thinking has transformed my life. That's one of the reasons I married the pony-tailed Presbyterian.

If we want to change the culture of the art institutions, if we want to change the culture of our inner lives, if we want to invite vulnerability, connection, and compassion into creative fields, I encourage you to look at your own artistic discipline. The future of the arts rests on artists achieving excellence without confusing our vitae with our value.

SELF-COACHING QUESTIONS

1. What moments besides salary negotiations make you question your worthiness?

2. How do you satisfy your ego when you're feeling insecure? Write down any thoughts you have that begin with "at least I . . ."

3. What messages are being sent in your art form about success? What practices might help us stop equating our work with our worth?

4. According to Brené Brown, courage, compassion, and connection are three things we do to practice worthiness. In your journal, write each of those three words on their own page. Make a list of activities, relationships, creative endeavors, and other things you are doing already that fall under each category. How courageous, compassionate, and connected do you feel? At the top of each page give yourself a score from 0 to 10.

5. Who do you know that needs reminding of their innate worthiness? Give them a call or send them a message telling them so now. Connection works both ways.

ÉTUDE: "IF ONLYS" AND THE INFORMATION THEY GIVE

Write down a couple of your "if only" statements and how you would feel if you'd accomplished them.

Example:

> *If only I had gone to a better college . . .*
> *If only the book were a* New York Times *best seller . . .*
> *If only I had more connections in this industry . . .*

Then I would feel . . .

> *Good about myself*
> *Accomplished*
> *Successful*

Next, mine these thoughts for dreams: What is at the heart of these desires?

> *I want to feel knowledgeable.*
> *I want to be a thought leader.*
> *I want to feel more connected and known.*

Now write down the fears that come up when you consider them.

Fears:

> *I am afraid I am not smart enough.*
> *I am afraid no one respects me.*
> *I am afraid I am a failure.*

Your turn: "If onlys"

1. If only I was . . .
2. If only I had . . .
3. If only it was . . .
4. If only there was . . .

If I achieved these or if these were true, then I would feel . . .

What dreams are at the heart of these desires?

What fears appear when you consider these dreams?

Cultivating an innate sense of worthiness takes practice. We need to have a bottom line for what we believe about our innate nature. Start by writing all the things that do not make you worthy.

Example:

Things that **do not** make me worthy:

> *Portfolio*
>
> *Resumé*
>
> *Success*
>
> *College degrees*
>
> *Awards*
>
> *Accolades*
>
> *How successful my children are*
>
> *How much money I make*
>
> *How fit I am*
>
> *How much I weigh*

Now, write what you believe about worthiness:

Worthiness words:

> *I am capable, even when I feel unqualified.*
> *I am whole, even when I feel lacking.*
> *I am worthy of love, even when I feel unlovable.*
> *I am worthy of respect, even when I feel I don't deserve it.*
> *I am enough, even when I want to change.*
> *I am good, even when I feel bad.*
> *My body is good, even if society tells me otherwise.*

Write more in your journal.

CODA ⊕

Value, as one of the seven elements of art, defines how light or dark a given color is. Maybe you've seen a value scale: the darkest black on one side, followed by very minute shade differences in each square until the last box is white. You start out with the darkest black, then move to charcoal, then to medium gray, then to light gray, and then to white, box by box. Value gives the appearance of texture and shadow in a photograph or painting. In fact, the word photograph comes from two Greek words that mean "light drawing." Value, then, is *how* the photograph portrays objects in light, using low or high contrast, that is, a lot of shades on a value scale or only a few. Regardless, it is the tonal values of the image that show us where the light is; how the artist renders value to depict an object greatly affects how it is perceived in a work of art.

In your own creative life, where does the light come from? In other words, what gives you your value? Are you going around and around trying to be the source of light yourself?

No wonder you're tired.

In your own creative life, where does the light come from? In other words, what gives you your value? Are you going around and around trying to be the source of light yourself? No wonder you're tired.

What would it be like to rest in the warmth of a light that is not yours to shine but just to see and be seen by? What more could you do with your energy if you knew you didn't have to earn your value? That everything about who you are, from light, to dark, to shades of gray, is merely a reflection of a truly benevolent light Source, and so just by your existence, your creation, regardless of what you achieve, you are given value? However you may define that light for yourself, whether it is within or without, I hope you'll remember to let it shine, to let it show you that you are living light drawing; invaluable, incredibly worthy, illuminating every darkness.

Five True Things (don't forget to add yours):

1. If no one is paying me to make art, it does not mean my art is worth zero dollars.

2. Cost and value are two different measuring sticks.

3. No job can define me as a sell-out or a success.

4. Practicing courage, compassion, and connection cultivates worthiness.

5.

FOURTEEN

Ode to Healing
The (Sometimes) Spiritual Path of Getting Unstuck

"Vocalise-étude," by Olivier Messiaen

Odd how the creative power at once brings the whole universe to order.

—Virginia Woolf, *The Diary of Virginia Woolf*

LILIANA

Every time she walks by the piano in her house, the grief slams the door to her heart shut. She'd been taking lessons again for the last few years.

That is, before her husband's cancer returned. He had been a music theorist and composer, and this was one of the reasons she'd fallen in love with him. Before they were married, she'd dreamt of having a house filled with music. When their children left for college, he had encouraged her to return to her own lessons. But when he got sick, she'd given it up. She'd had to.

With him gone, the piano lid and her love of music sat closed tightly in his studio. Of course, as her coach, I didn't know any of this in the first session with Liliana.

All she shared that day was, "I can't seem to feel motivated to practice."

"What kind of thoughts come up when you consider playing?" I asked.

"It's pointless. I'll probably die before I'm good enough to play Bach again. It's too late for me, I'm too old."

There's usually a payoff to staying stuck; Liliana's was avoiding the pain.

THE SKULL CATHEDRAL

I first attempted to turn my skull into a cathedral alone in a dingy practice room.

By now, you know that the creative life is full of metaphors. The oboe world was no exception. Throughout my training, everyone kept saying, "focus the air like you have a thumb over a garden hose," or "play with a ping pong ball or a jawbreaker candy inside your mouth." My teachers would tell me to "breathe through my feet," "inflate an imaginary balloon on the end of the oboe," or my personal favorite: "fill the skull cathedral with sound." I know now they were trying to get me to play with resonance, richness, and core. The most infuriating thing they said was, "You'll know it when you feel it."

It was not for lack of trying that my oboe tone was not resonant. Have you ever had someone tell you the same thing was wrong with you over and over and over? And lesson after lesson, when you hear, "You are *playing* wrong," there comes a point where, even for the toughest of us, it starts to sound like they are saying, "*You* are wrong." I remember lying awake and staring at the ceiling fan in my rented apartment and praying to a God I wasn't sure I believed in anymore, "Please, please, please . . . give me the secret."

In my coaching practice, I've seen so many artists in this kind of pain; they see where they want to be, have tried everything to get there, and after a certain point they begin to consider self-abandonment. They wonder if the last thing they will need to do to fix their art is to stop trusting their experience and deny themselves. They have tinkered with the instrument, posture, or embouchure so much that nothing works now. It feels foreign and wrong to create at all. The frustration of not being able to play with resonance for me became pain; the payoff to staying stuck was not having to face the existential crisis of self-doubt and shame that sat right next to the solution.

Toward the end of a long regular lesson, dozens of nonsensical metaphors later, things didn't seem any different. I felt the tears waiting behind my eyes. My teacher suggested we play a simple oboe duet; it is easier to resonate when playing with others. (There's another metaphor.)

I peered out the window at the students on the street below and took a breath. I looked down at the conglomeration of wood and metal in my hands. I thought of the weather patterns that made the cane of the reed dense and the tone rich. I considered asking for a break to collect myself, to disconnect from the moment. Sensing my discomfort, my teacher pointed to my oboe and said, *Sensing my discomfort, my teacher pointed to my oboe and said, "Let's put the emotion in here. The music can hold it."* "Let's put the emotion in here. The music can hold it."

As we harmonized, a mysterious third note suddenly appeared in my ear. Since oboes can only play one note at a time, hearing someone else playing in the room made me stop and look around, perplexed. It sounded low, buzzy, and faint like someone had forgotten about the dog under the piano who was now growling along.

My teacher laughed in that gregarious way he did in these moments of discovery. This third note, or what others might call a difference or resultant tone, was an otoacoustic emission. It was not coming from the instruments themselves (or some secret studio dog), but from a listener's inner ear. If that duet with my teacher had been recorded, for example, you wouldn't have seen the third voice we were hearing on the waveform audio, even though it was detectable if you were in the room with us. The computer doesn't have a human inner ear. The whole of these two notes we played was greater than the sum of their parts.

My teacher and I locked eyes. The oboe reed, my jaw, the inside of my mouth, the air behind the reed, all of it aligned. Somehow, my skull *did* feel like a cavernous room as the sound—*my* sound—connected somehow to my core while soaring upward to the highest heavens, one might even call it a "skull cathedral." It resonated more deeply than anything I'd ever heard or felt. I was hooked.

IF YOU'RE STILL STUCK

There are many reasons not to create. We've explored many in this book. Throughout these chapters, we've worked with our mindset and our schedule, and we've learned ways to overcome rejection and find our people. For some, this work will have felt spiritual all along. But what if, thirteen chapters later, you still feel unmotivated, uninspired, and inexplicably blocked? Sometimes, the solution is as simple as waking up earlier or shifting the lens. Other times, we climb a long staircase only to find a locked door.

Consistently showing up to our creative vulnerability takes courage. Especially when right next to the creative goals we set are trigger points for pain—in the form of fear, grief, or shame. But the physics of resonance, the third voice, reminds us that we do not create in a vacuum. We are not alone in the creative act, even when we find pain there. When we create, we tune into the universe, the quote attributed to Einstein goes. Each creative step we take speaks beyond us or perhaps in spite of us. Music-making and all creative vibrations resonate through the skull cathedrals of our own minds and into the heart; they spread and pulsate, forever altering the environment. The art can hold our pain.

In my journey to the skull cathedral, when the third voice appeared as I first started to resonate, I learned that the creative act is, at its heart, connection. Connection with self, with each other, and something larger than ourselves. Creativity helps us heal when we harmonize with that third voice.

TELLING THE TRUTH

In James Baldwin's essay, "Notes of a Native Son," he wrote, "I imagine one of the reasons people cling to their hate so stubbornly is because they sense, once hate is gone, they will be forced to deal with pain."

That quote struck like a lightning bolt when I first read it. In Baldwin's original connotation, pain lurks beneath the racism so steeped in hate. Whenever trauma, grief, or despondency is masked with hate, it can make one feel powerful. While written in 1963, Baldwin's words now ring truer than ever: what lies underneath our rejection and disconnection with ourselves and others is pain. The hatred can be self-directed, too. Have you hidden yourself from anguish with muted self-hatred? Have you participated in self-erasure in an effort to run from failure, distress, and shame?

In light of my search for a resonant oboe sound, Baldwin's words left me asking myself, *What else am I clinging to out of avoidance and fear of pain?* Sometimes, it is so much easier to stay creatively blocked, not to make the poem or the music, to not sit down at the piano and wipe the dust away. There seems to be pain under every rock that needs moving; no wonder we cling to our blocks. This kind of discomfort and numbness feels familiar. Add in the glorification of creative suffering, the tortured-artist myth, and the block becomes a mountain. We start to believe it is who we are.

But here's the good news: great art moves mountains. It does that by exposing us to ourselves, even if we aren't writing a memoir or painting a self-portrait. We've learned that vulnerability is the antidote to perfectionism, which means bringing to light the pain underneath the self-hatred, fear, or imposter syndrome thoughts. Making something I care about can require me to face the reality of all that I do not know and cannot yet do, and yet creativity is the very catalyst that helps me learn, grow, shift, and heal. But we must keep trying, keep showing up.

But here's the good news: great art moves mountains.

One of my favorite authors, Rachel Held Evans, kept a sticky note above her desk, that said, "tell the truth." We, artists, prefer to stay stuck in the echo chamber of our own inner voices, telling us we are not good enough, because some days that seems easier than the alternative; letting go and finding out whether those voices are right, experiencing the fall-out that comes with exposing the system, of telling the truth.

We forget that even though the creative process can bring pain to the surface, it also invites us to do something with it, to walk through it clear to the other side.

OPEN THE LID

Liliana told me recently, through working in one of our creative recovery groups, that she realized it wasn't her age keeping her from taking piano lessons and practicing again. Of course, it was the grief. It was anger. Missing him didn't hurt so much with the piano lid closed.

A few months later, after she had cleaned out his closet and the rest of his office, she knew it was time to go to the piano. The Steinway was cluttered with scores and textbook drafts that he was editing before he fell ill. She started by removing all the papers from the sides of the music stand and finally sat down and opened the lid.

To her surprise, she found a light green sticky note on middle C. His handwriting read, "If you want to get better, you're going to have to open the lid." He must have written it before the last hospital stay.

Underneath her block, underneath that lid, was immense pain and regret, but she stayed seated there and began to play. Through her tears, she plunked out a simple Bach Two-Part Invention she knew by heart, and then it appeared. Joy washed over her. His note was a synchronicity, a third voice, reminding her she was loved and not alone.

Creativity can sometimes take us to the center of our pain. And maybe, for you, pain looks like rage or disinterest or procrastination. Overcoming these blocks often requires us to enter the land where metaphors fail. It is a spiritual path. But, as Virigina Woolf wrote, we must not forget that the creative power "brings the whole universe to order." Waiting there when we strike the key, paint the canvas, and begin the climb to the skull cathedral, we will ultimately find connection, resonance, and healing. Making things gives us a place to put our pain; when we do, the world vibrates sympathetically. Opening the lid alters the inner ear of creation.

THE VOICE OF YOUR HEART

After the lesson where I first heard the third voice, I never wanted to play any other way again. Of course, I did continue to play without resonance, that is, until I learned to find the way back to the skull cathedral myself. Eventually, it became easier, and in the years since that day, through a creative devotion routine, my oboe sound has become the voice of my heart. When I share music with anyone, even an empty room, it puts into waveform the pain, but also the joy.

I invite you on your own journey to your own skull cathedral. It is a solitary one, but we aren't alone. May you find the comfort and courage you need to create despite the pain you know lies underneath the blocks that keep you stuck. May you listen for the third voice sounding in the form of whatever synchronicities or "God winks" your creative vibrations may trigger. May they be the healing balm for a whole world of weariness.

The ancient Greeks wrote of what they called "the music of the spheres," naming the proportions found in the movements of celestial bodies—the Sun, Moon, and planets—as a form of music. They believed the universe was a harmonious place, singing as it spun. What if, when you read the story, share the painting, or take the audition, you harmonize with a universe that has been singing since the beginning of time? The only thing missing is your own heart's voice. The song isn't the same without you. In the face of pain, name it. Then have the courage to fill the skull cathedral, open the lid, create anyway. Listen for it to resonate with a mystery beyond words. You will know it when you feel it.

What if, when you read the story, share the painting, or take the audition, you harmonize with a universe that has been singing since the beginning of time? The only thing missing is your own heart's voice. The song isn't the same without you. In the face of pain, name it. Then have the courage to fill the skull cathedral, open the lid, create anyway. Listen for it to resonate with a mystery beyond words. You will know it when you feel it.

SELF-COACHING QUESTIONS

1. How are you benefiting from staying creatively blocked? What pain might be hiding underneath your block(s)?

2. Creativity is one resource for healing. What are others?

3. What synchronicities have you experienced in your life in general? Any while reading this book?

4. What do you believe about the existence of a Higher Power? How do these beliefs inform your creative life?

5. Who do you discuss spiritual or philosophical topics with? Do you feel accepted and seen in these interactions?

ÉTUDE: NAME YOUR CREATIVE IMPULSE METAPHOR

Choose a metaphor for your creative impulse. Below are some examples, but make sure you choose your own. Naming our creative impulse metaphor does a couple of things for us. First, it separates our creative work from our identity, reminding us that we are not what we create. Second, this process should feel playful and fun, allowing your inner child to reflect on a slightly mysterious, indescribable, and joyful process.

Creativity is . . .

Simmering sauce

Planting seeds

A rainbow after a storm

A dog chasing squirrels

Giving birth

Turning my skull into a cathedral

Bungee jumping

What resonates with you about the metaphor you chose? Does it feel like a different metaphor in different art forms? Has it felt different at other points in your life or stage in your development? Name the lens which lies under your metaphor. Return to the étude in chapter 10 for tips on shifting your lens if needed.

CODA ⊕

The first images from the James Webb Space Telescope were shared with the public in July 2022. You remember: the cosmos's brilliant blues and oranges, that star-sparkle truly otherworldly, spellbinding, not to mention the mind-bending time-traveling the viewer of those photographs was experiencing.

The *New York Times* suddenly read like a sci-fi novella:

> To look outward into space is to peer into the past. Light travels at a constant 186,000 miles per second, or close to six trillion miles per year, through the vacuum of space. To observe a star 10 light-years away is to see it as it existed 10 years ago, when the light left its surface. The farther away a star or galaxy lies, the older it is, making every telescope a kind of time machine.
>
> "That was always out there," said Jane Rigby, an astrophysicist at NASA's Goddard Space Flight Center and the telescope's operations manager. "We just had to build a telescope to go see what was there."

What more is there to see in your creative life? Those pictures of space are just one minuscule snapshot of a vast cosmos, one glimpse of stars that are ten light-years away, whose likeness has likely changed by now, the fleeting seasons of stars as they burn, and so what if it is similar with you?

What if your creative practice is the telescope you can build to show you everything that has always been in you all along?

What if your creative practice is the telescope you can build to show you everything that has always been in you all along?

Here's the most amazing thing—we feel kindred with the stars because we are made of the same dust. Let it remind us of all that is discoverable within us then, and let our creativity be the exploratory work that stretches time, making us somehow believe again, shining the light of hope in the face of the darkest black-hole seasons of our lives, like a north star we can follow straight on to morning.

Five True Things (what's yours?):

1. When I cast my art into the world, I connect to something larger than myself.

2. A trigger is a wound calling out to be healed.

3. The art can hold the pain.

4. When something is wrong with my technique, it doesn't change my innate worthiness.

5.

FIFTEEN

Ode to Joy
The Artist's Oath

Adagio in E-Flat, by Tison Street

The human soul doesn't want to be advised or fixed or saved.
It simply wants to be witnessed.
> —Parker Palmer, "Misgivings About Advice"

ELLE

Elle was a highly exhibited, award-winning, long-CV kind of artist. She came to me completely blocked. In her introductory email, she wrote, "I am clearly creative, but I have no idea where my creative self is. Maybe she's in the mountains, and I've been looking for her at the beach?" (Even when struggling, Elle always has this lightheartedness about her.)

The basic issue with her was that she was a visual artist who refused to enter her studio. *Refused* may be too strong a word. It was less dramatic and more perplexing than that: she just didn't want to go in there and work. It had been four years since she had made any art. There was no single reason, many little ones, maybe.

Yet in the end, even after we moved each obstacle from her path—the roof (damaged in a storm) was repaired, the walls repainted, the shelves rebuilt and organized, and exhibitions rescheduled—she *still* wasn't making. She was no longer drawn to that physical space and worried that maybe this meant she wasn't an artist anymore.

ORCHESTRA ETIQUETTE

> *Early is on time, and on time is late.*
> *Absolutely NO perfume.*
> *Black socks only.*
> *At the first rehearsal, be performance ready.*
> *Always bring a pencil.*
> *No cell phones.*
> *Don't tap your feet.*
> *Don't tune loudly.*
> *Don't play too much while others are tuning.*
> *Don't turn around and look at people behind you during rehearsal.*
> *Don't speak to the conductor unless he/she speaks to you first.*
> *If something is out of tune, assume it is you.*

These are just a few spoken and unspoken codes of conduct in the orchestra world. If you are a classical musician, you likely learned them from the first day of band or orchestra. Even now, I leave abnormally early for a gig to be in my seat at least thirty minutes before the baton drops. I can't shake it—these codes of conduct were ingrained in me from a young age.

As with any institution steeped in tradition, every creative practice comes with its own rules of the road. Many of them make good sense, some even protect us. They keep us from being overworked or mistreated, help us respect one another and the work we do together, they make for a nice work environment.

But what happens when these ways of being bleed over into our own individual creative process? What happens when they restrict us or stop us from taking chances or shifting our mindset? For example, what kind of "work environment" is there in your head when you are writing that rough draft?

So much of my work seeking a resonant creative life has been about unraveling these rules, setting my own ways of being, separate from what I learned in school or on the job so far. One rule that I've learned to break is being dually careered. During my conservatory training, I learned that when you make money doing something besides playing your instrument, it's because you don't make enough playing music. For years, I felt the itch for more in my life and denied myself joy. So even calling myself a *writer* breaks the codes I was taught. The "and" was a liability; the multi-faceted life as an artist was frowned upon. When we internalize beliefs like this, how could they not affect our mindset?

Have you ever taken the time to watch your patterns and thoughts when you are creating? How do you speak to yourself about it? When you are fleshing out this or that idea while you are waiting for inspiration to hit, when you are trying to find the energy to get to work in the first place—what are the rules you are living by? What codes of conduct protect you from going too long without a break or withstanding the toxic self-talk?

When I'm coaching people struggling with their mindset or creative block, I see them fighting the same fight. So many of us need help redefining what the language we use truly means. We need new definitions of words like *success* or, in Elle's case, *studio*.

This is where we found her breakthrough. I asked her what she used to feel like in the studio before she was blocked, and she retorted without hesitation, "It used to feel like what I imagine my dog feels on her walk. Every rock, every leaf, every tree is a delight: the world is just one big, sweet-smelling possibility." From here, I led her through a lens exercise I learned in my coaching training (which inspired the étude at the end of chapter 10), and we walked through a couple of different lenses that could help her see her studio differently. We looked at Elle's issue with the studio through the lens of:

- a puppy;
- herself at age eight;
- an ambassador.

The last one was most generative. Her eyes lit up, "Ambassadors are sent out. They are citizens of the world. Maybe the studio is more than the four walls and a roof!" She was nearly screaming with joy.

So, as every foreign servant does at the beginning of their service, I asked Elle to craft an oath to take. Ambassadors promise "to defend the constitution from all its enemies foreign and domestic," and so, looking at her studio through that lens, what was Elle promising to defend? I asked her to name what she believed about the studio, about her creative life, to state the code of conduct, and list the agreements about how she would approach herself and her work—that was her assignment, and she came back the next week glowing and eager to share.

As I listened attentively, she named the most powerful thing: "The studio is *life*; I am always in my studio."

Where previously stood a big creative block, words and creative joy came pouring out. We both teared up as everything she wrote sounded true. Something in her had changed.

Her creative impulse rebounded unbelievably fast. She started a new project based on found objects from the forest where she walks her dog. She brought the *studio* back into the four walls of her workspace. She was healing and it was an honor to be a witness to her progress and growth.

After that session, I knew I had to write my own vow to my creative self; what I want my inner artist to know is true, a code of conduct, a pledge, affirmation, or word of honor. I hope my oath will inspire you to write your own.

MY ARTIST'S OATH

I joyfully swear . . .

- to keep showing up. Even when I wonder if I am a great big fake or a complete hack;

- to be gentle with myself, to offer loving kindness to myself and others, because creating is a lot like becoming a mother—it can be painful, messy, and make you question your whole identity;

- to forgive myself for my perceived mistakes or failures, read them like a map, believing each one has something to teach me;

- to allow myself to grieve these losses, to offer myself grace and understanding, compassion and release around every embarrassment, missed mark, lost audition, or email pitch that was not responded to.

Code of Conduct

- I will not starve myself, literally or figuratively.

- I do not have to earn my shower.

- No matter how hard I do or do not work, I will first and foremost take care of my physical and mental health because the instrument is me.

- I will pursue my Inner Artist and parent my Inner Child with love.

- I will find time for play, "fill the form" (Julia Cameron) with rest, laughter, and connection.

- I will ride my routines like a life raft, remembering I have the right to change the routine when it no longer works.

- I will tell the truth, lean into vulnerability, cultivate "thick skin, tender heart" (Rachel Held Evans).

- I will be direct about my needs and desires with myself and others, believing "clear is kind" (Brené Brown) I know that needing or wanting something doesn't make me weak.

- I will protect my energy, guard myself from crazy makers and toxic people who snuff out my light and suck up my joy.

- I will hear my life by witnessing my thoughts with regularity.

- I will not believe everything I think.

- I will see procrastination for what it is: fear. I will love myself through every fear.

- I will keep trying to find "the angel in the marble" (Michelangelo). I will remember that it is hard work that sets her free, and that that process is reductive, only a matter of letting things go to reveal all that is already hidden within.

- I will look for ways to be a beginner again, to stop judging myself when I am starting or starting over.

- I will stop giving people I don't even like control over my actions or feelings, to constantly evaluate and reevaluate whose criticism I will take to heart.

- I will see my identity as an empath as a strength instead of a liability; to know my tenderness and openness to feeling is a superpower for compassion, connection, and creativity.

- I will remember that the tortured-artist stereotype is a lie, that great art can come from joy as well as pain and suffering.

- I will eat vegetables and drink water.

- I will listen to all that my jealousy, anger, anxiety, and triggers are trying to teach me. I will let them call to all that needs healing, all that I want, all that my life is singing to me.

- I will know that my worthiness does not come from a salary number or office size, from a title or an accolade, that no matter what I achieve, it will never be enough, and the only thing that will fit in the God-sized hole in my heart is God. Or as C. S. Lewis puts it, "If I find in myself a desire which no experience in this world can satisfy, the most probable explanation is that I was made for another world."

- I will spend my life living into Madeleine L'Engle's words, that "the discipline of creation . . . is an effort towards wholeness," and know, therefore, that nothing is wasted.

- I will answer the invitation to another world that creativity offers with a resounding "Yes, and . . .," surrendering to the Spirit's restoration of my soul through play.

- I will rest knowing that I am one of the "ones" the Good Shepherd has been after, beloved and whole.

- I will let myself be loved and seen, forgiven and healed through the creative act and know that even when that is painful and vulnerable, I am never alone.

I dedicate this oath to artists everywhere, that I might serve them, help them overcome blocks both foreign and domestic, both internal and external, to help them sing their song, to change their lens, to not give up. May they open the studio doors wide and see (as Julia Cameron says) that life is a date with their inner artist, that all of creation is just one big masterpiece and they are each a unique and irreplaceable part of it.

Whereas the party, one Merideth Hite Estevez, signs hereto, on this day, with joy.

Will you be a witness?

SELF-COACHING QUESTIONS

1. How do the actions in your life reflect your deeply held beliefs?

2. What beliefs of others have you found most inspiring? Harmful?

3. Do you associate your creative practice with a particular physical space? Describe it.

4. What unspoken or spoken ways of being are there in your art form? Do you uphold these with joy or begrudgingly?

5. Who in your life can you ask to witness your oath signing? Who can *you* stand as an accountability partner for?

ÉTUDE: YOUR ARTIST'S OATH

Now it's time to write your own oath. There is no set prescription for this process. This is a binding agreement between you and yourself, so it is yours to shape. In some ways, you've been writing your oath since chapter 1. Flip back to your journal with your étude responses and use the heart words from chapter 6 and the lenses you wanted to name from chapter 10, include your Why (for Now) from chapter 11, and your creative impulse metaphor for chapter 14, et cetera. Here are a few questions to guide you:

- What do you "joyfully swear"? What promises feel important to keep?

- Code of Conduct: How do you want to show up? What do you want always to do or sometimes do? What things are prohibited?

- Name any challenges and helpful lenses from the étude at the end of chapter 10 and explore how you'd like to respond to them specifically.

- Who is this oath for? Who isn't it for? What wise words from any "artist saints" do you want to remember, and what quotes or memories that you want to shape how you treat yourself and others?

True Things: Pull all the true things you wrote from each chapter and write them in one spot in your études journal. Use them in your oath. When you're done writing your oath, make space for your signature and the signature of a witness. As you witness others' oaths, remember Parker Palmer's words—"The human soul doesn't want to be advised or fixed or saved. It simply wants to be witnessed." Share with a friend when you're ready. Put your oath somewhere you can see it.

CODA ⊕

The world argues over much, but protecting the elegant, mysterious, majestic sea turtles is something we mostly agree on. Sea turtles are said to have been around for 110 million years, basically since the age of the dinosaurs. Beyond being one of the oldest species on Earth, these reptiles happen to be my favorite animal. Most of them live to be over a hundred years old. They cry real tears because of all the sea salt.

They swim thousands of miles through the ocean to migrate back to the same beach to lay eggs. For example, the Pacific Loggerhead turtle swims over 7,500 miles from Japan to Mexico.

Scientists aren't even sure how these creatures navigate the ocean to find their way back. One theory is magnetoreception, a special sense they believe turtles use to read the Earth's magnetic field as they swim to their home beach.

What if your call to create was meant to bring you home to your true self?

What if your call to create was meant to bring you home to your true self?

I believe we have a sense as artists, our own magnetic compass of sorts, that helps us on our way. Maybe the noise of the world or everybody's expectations or your own failures or secret shame tend to send you swimming in some other direction, but that does not mean you won't return to who you truly are. It's the opening theme you will never forget. When we live in congruence with what we believe to be true, even when it is 8,000 miles away, so to speak, we can return. We can swim back. Our creativity connects us to the way.

It can feel vulnerable; even sea turtles can't go inside their shells. Sometimes, being one who feels so deeply can be exhausting. But returning to what you've named throughout this book as true, what you write in your oath that you promise to yourself, let these words be the magnetic signature of your home beach.

Create space to get alone and quiet long enough to listen to your life as it calls to you. And, please, for the love of all things beautiful, enjoy the journey. Let no one begrudge you your path; it is uniquely yours.

And remember, you have your own committee behind you, protecting you. I, for one, will fight to ensure artists' voices are heard over all that threatens us, and I will work to make our needs known. I won't stop coming after each one. Like the sea turtles, the cave paintings, and all other miracles of creation remind us: beauty resonates beyond what we can see or even dream of.

And you and I get to sing along.

Turn and swim toward home now.

Finale: Fugue

Joy is getting to the end and realizing it's just the beginning.

In the final movement of the symphony that is your life, you find what sounds like a new theme appearing. When you listen closely, there are echoes of something from the opening, but something about this is different. It is a truer version. This journey was, in some ways, painful. Themes were broken apart.

Now, hearing this finale, you realize they were not being broken apart but broken open. The brilliant and innocent opening is mixed with the poignancy of the tumultuous middle, like broken pottery etched with gold. This end is broader, surer of itself, resonating with rightness.

This time, the theme repeats right away, in a different voice, then again in a different octave. The soundscape is suddenly saturated with every shade, transposed to this timbre then that, turned on its head playfully, the long, drawn-out notes in the middle voices—you suddenly realize, it's been your theme all along. Just when you think it is done spinning, the whirling continues. Everything you see in this score reverberates with a joy that is wholly and completely yours.

YOU WERE BORN FOR MORE THAN GOOD

This book is a love letter to you, dear one. All the things you are, whatever the ways the world has broken you, seduced you with good when you were born for so much

> *We need the creative offerings within you that only you can bring forth, but more than that, more than anything you make, the world needs* **you.**

more, may you see it all now for the mosaic that it is, not for sale, reflecting light with all the colors in it. We need the creative offerings within you that only you can bring forth, but more than that, more than anything you make, the world needs *you.*

What I didn't know about creative recovery when I started, what I find most powerful about it now, was that it would lead to a deeper healing of more than my relationship with my oboe. I know now that creativity is how we learn, heal, explore, and play, all rolled into one. It is how we *are.* No wonder kids create with such ease and joy. When we deny ourselves the pleasure of making things we care about, we lose more than artistic development; we lose touch with something true, hidden deep inside of us.

These are valuable tools, not just for artists. And yet, in light of the tortured-artist myth and how a culture so often glorifies or even fetishizes artists' suffering, it can be difficult for artists to recover their sense of self or mental and physical health. They start to believe that being mentally unstable or physically sick is the cost of having talent.

And if you take away one thing from this book, let it be this: if your creative practice costs you your joy in life, the cost is too great. Cultivating a joyful, creative life is possible, but it takes intentionality, time, and lots and lots of grace. It takes a willingness to show up to do the work on yourself, just like you practice your scales or edit the draft. It means being open to the spiritual shifts you can't see coming. It isn't easy, but these roads lead to more than increased productivity or optimum health. I have seen them transform relationships and save people's lives. In my own story, this work has made everything vibrate with a resonance that I now call joy—my marriage, mothering, and daily life.

As many metaphors as I've used in this book to describe how "being well" and finding joy feels, in the end, you must set out for the skull cathedral yourself. Know that when you choose to love your inner artist, be about the work of forgiveness and worthiness, and live with heart, you'll notice parts of your life that you'd forgotten existed begin to vibrate sympathetically. This is what it means to feel imperfectly whole.

Take the theme of joy you were born with and transpose it playfully. Live your life live. Enjoying the process far more than the product. Be developed and return home to yourself every chance you get. But for now, strike the chord. And as you make the art, listen for all your life is saying to you in the reverb. Lift the pedal and let it ring.

Bonus Étude: Curtain Call Questions—How to Be Done

With each book you write, you die, and you're born again.
—Madeleine L'Engle, *A Circle of Quiet*

Azucena Estevez was born and raised in Guatemala, and she immigrated to Plainfield, New Jersey, at twenty-three. She also happens to be my mother-in-law. When I gave birth to my daughter Eva, La Mami (her nickname translates to mean "The Mommy" in Spanish) came to give me *la cuarentena*, or the forty days.

In Guatemalan culture, someone spends forty days with a woman who has just given birth. They believe that new mothers need just as much care as newborns. La Mami stayed by my side and behind the scenes taking care of everything when Eva was born. She prepared breakfast, lunch, and dinner for me. She did all the laundry. She washed the bottles and the pump parts. She afforded my husband and me a blissful three-hour chunk of sleep. She mothered me so I could mother Eva. She did the same three-and-a-half years later when I had my son, Eli. This was the greatest gift anyone has ever given me.

When I finished writing the first draft of this book, I closed the computer and looked around. Expecting to feel ecstatic, it slowly dawned on me what was next: the feedback, the red-penned revisions, the fact that people

I know (and don't know) would read this thing (that is, if I'm lucky). Now that the book was written and no longer existed as some nebulous thing in my brain, the verdict was in: it was and would never be perfect. I felt exhausted, exuberant, relieved, and full of dread at the same time. The feeling of being done can be a creative block in and of itself.

Regardless of what metaphor you choose to represent your creative impulse, whether or not you have given birth to a human from your body, you can guess that making art and giving birth to human babies are not exactly the same. But they both take an incredible amount of time and hard work. The creator could benefit from care and compassion once the job is done.

Just like at the end of the show when the actor returns to take their bow no matter how small their role, receive applause and appreciation from yourself regardless of how you performed. Ask yourself these questions when you finish something.

THE CURTAIN CALL QUESTIONS

1   Celebrate: What and how will you celebrate?

2   Grieve: What do you need to grieve? What do you wish had been different?

3   Notice: What synchronicities showed up? What surprised you? If you are a person of faith, ask: Where did God show up in this work?

4   Hope: What hopes do you have now? What prayer or wish do you send future "ones" who will experience your art?

ÉTUDE: *LA CUARENTENA*—A RITUAL FOR BEING DONE

Just like postpartum anxiety and depression are very real, all kinds of feelings come up for us when things we have worked hard to put our heart and soul into end, released from our hands. After playing the show or submitting the manuscript, your bad mood or melancholy state could be your inner artist calling out for you to notice them and give them the love and support they need. Proceed gently with yourself as things end and new things begin.

Proceed gently with yourself as things end and new things begin.

As an act of celebration and self-care, create your own ritual of *la cuarentena*—can you give yourself forty hours away from the manuscript before editing? Can you spend $40 on something you've been wanting? Can you write a list of forty things you are grateful for? There is nothing magic about the number forty, mind you. It has its roots in ancient scriptures, like when God spoke to Moses on a mountaintop and Jesus fasted in the desert. What matters about these rituals is giving yourself the gift of time. If Madeleine L'Engle was right and with each project we die and are reborn, then time for deep rest, reflection, and listening—to your body, life, and spirit—is a must. Watch for the joy that is close at hand.

Create your own ritual for being done with this book. You've earned it.

Acknowledgments

When I lived in NYC, I used to sit on a rock in Central Park that I deemed my "prayer rock." Through some of the most painful years of my creative life, I would lie on the rock, look at the sky, and ask God, "Why?" An Artist-God makes the broken beautiful, and this book is that.

Without my family's help, I might have never left that rock. I'm especially grateful to my husband, Edwin, who first gave me *The Artist's Way* and encouraged me to find community with it. Thank you for dancing with the giant stuffed bear, teaching our children to love sunsets, and making me record the random songs you make up. Thank you, Eva and Eli, for your joy. It calls me home.

To Azucena "La Mami" Estevez, who selflessly pours herself out on my behalf. I hit the mother-in-law jackpot; this book would not exist without her help. How fitting that it comes out so close to your birthday! (Don't worry, this isn't your gift.)

To my parents, Tommy and Deb Hite, who made it safe for me to be myself. To my grandparents, who did everything from teaching me to read to paying for my education. To my siblings, Heather, Tombo, and Mack, for their friendship and unconditional love.

To my forever English teacher, Margaret Jameson, who first believed in my writing even though I chose to pen a persuasive essay about why everyone should play the oboe. (Which convinced zero people, for the record.) Thank you for loving me like a daughter and teaching me grammar.

Thank you to my literary agent, Don Pape, who spoils his writers by responding to texts within minutes. To my editors Lil Copan, Lisa Kloskin, Diedre Hammons, and everyone at Broadleaf for shepherding this first-time author gracefully through the process.

To Quinn Simpson and McKenzie Cerri, co-founders of Graydin, whose Start with Heart model shifted everything I thought I knew about coaching.

To those whose stories inspired this book: Nicole Joseph, Geena Flores, Jim Moseley, Vanesa Simon, Emily Pastor, Lorrie Fredette, Audra Ziegel, and countless other coaching clients, friends, and loved ones who chose to remain anonymous.

As the Artists for Joy Creative Clusters have grown, my facilitator friends always have my back, especially as I took the time to write this book. Thank you, Jill Benfield, Theresa Clarke, Vanesa Simon, David James, Sara McMahon, Angela Sheik, Trina Drotar, Jessi Rosinski, Johanna Burian, David Westerlund, and Toni Lovejoy for making space for creatives to feel seen and supported and for reminding me to play.

To my coach-turned-friend Ann Kroeker, for her patient listening and endless generosity with her time, energy, and sentence solutions. This book is here because of you!

To Ariel Curry of Hungry Authors, who helped me get clear on the transformation of this book and answered many requests for subhead and chapter title ideas at the eleventh hour.

SDG

Creative Recovery Community Guide

If you've found this book helpful in reclaiming your joy, perhaps you'd like to facilitate creative recovery groups in your community. Consider this section a gathering guide. Julia Cameron deemed these groups "Creative Clusters," and this work can be done in art schools, music conservatories, spiritual communities, book clubs, or any place you find creatives looking for support and connection. This book has fifteen weeks of content, which fits nicely into an average semester timeline or the distance between Labor Day and Christmas or February to May. Below are more suggestions for using the book with others and general ideas for facilitating meaningful conversations.

Connection is key for feeling worthy, but being in community with other artists is enormously fun, too. As the lead facilitator of Creative Clusters with Artists for Joy since 2017, I have led thousands of artists in creative recovery and discovery and I wrote this book with these powerful gatherings in mind.

MAKE THE SPACE SAFE

We begin each cohort by asking participants to read and agree to the following disclaimer (feel free to borrow ours or write your own):

Language matters: Whoever you are, wherever you come from, regardless of your experience or ability level, you are welcome here.

Help us welcome everyone by:

- Naming your experience without making assumptions about others.

- Creating space for all voices to be heard. (Hang back if you share often or nudge yourself forward if you have yet to share, as you're comfortable!)

- Never use language that is racist, sexist, homophobic, transphobic, ableist, classist, or xenophobic, as it will not be tolerated at Artists for Joy events.

Creativity is soul-work: Be gentle with yourself and others as you discover and recover your creative impulse. Conversations around creativity can touch on topics that are loaded for some, like spirituality, identity, or even trauma. Name what you need and make space for others to do the same. Never give unsolicited advice; the simple act of listening is incredibly powerful.

Have fun: There is an energy when a gaggle of fellow creative spirits comes together. It's seriously the best thing ever. So, let the joy spill over when it comes. You aren't too late. You aren't out of time. You are right where you need to be. Here is your permission slip to enjoy yourself.

Speak up: The facilitators are here to help. Do not be afraid to ask them questions by directly messaging them in the chat or emailing your facilitator. Please report any concerns or questions directly to them; we will help however we can.

FACILITATE, DON'T TEACH

The art of facilitation is creative in and of itself. It also takes practice. The following ideas are a conglomeration of all I have learned in my coaching training through Graydin and summers at Teaching Artist training through Lincoln Center Education, using Maxine Green's groundbreaking Aesthetic Education Curriculum.

When you bring artists together in a community, see your role not as an instructor or expert/keeper of all knowledge but as someone who makes space for others to explore topics, ask questions, and experience belonging. As a facilitator, make it your goal to ask more than you tell. Pauses are okay; learn to love silence.

THE RIGHT QUESTIONS AT THE RIGHT TIME

- Begin with "What?" or "How?" and avoid "Why?" (Graydin "deems asking 'why' to be ineffective because it often encourages defensiveness . . . and tends to narrow . . . thinking.")

- Try open questions that require more than "yes" or "no" answers.

- Consider the scope of a question; make it invitational but not prying.

- Consider the idea of "lasting questions"—rhetorical questions people can explore in their morning pages or self-reflection time.

- Curiosity is contagious: try "I wonder . . ."

- "What do you notice?" makes a great invitation as you view a work of art.

- "What resonates with you?" allows people to claim their own experience.

LISTEN, HEAR, PAUSE, MIRROR

The power of deeply listening to another and resisting the temptation to give them advice or direction is a potent skill for community building and connection. Model this as a facilitator by responding to a participant's sharing by pausing, acknowledging them, and, if it feels appropriate, mirroring back their statement with "What I hear you saying . . ." Another simple thing to add after someone shares is: "Thank you so much for sharing that with us." Resist the temptation to add your thoughts, share your experience, or offer your advice or opinion on their circumstances. Believing each participant has the answers within them to find their unique path empowers them to do so while feeling supported by others. Encourage artists to take better care of themselves by offering resources for cost-effective or free mental and behavioral health, as well as addiction recovery outlets. Do the work to research these resources before your first meeting and consider posting them somewhere participants can return to them as needed.

LOGISTICS

Artists for Joy Creative Clusters meet online weekly for fifteen weeks. We break our time into three half-hour segments, which we call Acts, totaling ninety minutes. Act I is spent gathering as a large group. We post an opening question and play simple music to help people transition into a creative and reflective posture. The host facilitator leads a short warm-up activity or discussion around a work of art or a topic from the chapter. After about twenty-five minutes, participants break out into groups of three or four, for Act II. The self-coaching questions at the end of each chapter make for a good start for a small group discussion, but participants are encouraged to introduce themselves and discuss the reading, using the prompts as needed to spark conversation. We remind participants to be mindful of their "airtime" and empower others to speak as they feel comfortable. We return to the larger group after another half hour in breakout rooms (some call them "breakthrough" rooms), and the last thirty minutes (or Act III) are spent doing and/or discussing the chapter's étude together. When we finish each of the book's three parts, we reflect on the experience of Exposition, Development, and Recapitulation as a whole. Finally, the last three to five minutes of each meeting are set apart for "closing words," marking time together and ending in a shared ritual. See below for some examples.

Since many artists have perfectionistic tendencies, reassure them that there is no perfect way to read this or any book. Whether or not you read every word of the chapter that week, whatever activities you could try, in Artists for Joy Creative Clusters, all are welcome to come as they are. There is no gold star or to-do list with hearing your life; it is the consistent desire to show up to do so that makes all the difference.

SPACE-MAKING

Rituals create a sense of group identity and foster belonging. They build trust, cooperation, teamwork, and communication. It softens transitions and helps us connect on a deeper level. When prompts or actions are short, it allows the group to hear many voices in a short time.

RITUALS FOR BEGINNING AND ENDINGS

1. In a word, share what you are feeling about embarking on a creative recovery journey and then follow it with "I'm in."

2. Participants share a short struggle or creative challenge and everyone in the group responds in unison with "*[Person's Name]*, I've got your back."

3. Participants share a worry they have and everyone in the group responds in unison "God's* got this."

4. Read through the list of True Things at the end of each chapter together, allowing the voices to overlap. (This is extremely powerful to do in online meetings with unmuted mics.)

5. Ask participants to share a true thing of their own in the chat during online meetings.

6. From Graydin: Ask "What are you bringing into this space today?" Offer a short visualization for participants, having them imagine carrying a heavy load into the meeting and invite them to physically put the baggage down somewhere safe outside.

---

* Feel free to invite participants to exchange whatever word resonates with them: "You've got this" or "Love's got this" are two examples we use in our groups. It can be very powerful to have participants use whatever words they want in a Greek chorus of compassion and support.

Music Makes Everything Better

Below is a link and QR code to the music I've made and collected for you. At the opening of each chapter, I list a track from *The Artist's Joy* playlist that goes along with the text from that section. When you click, you will also find playlists with music from my award-winning podcast and music we use during the Artists for Joy Creative Cluster gatherings. I hope you'll feel me cheering you on toward creative joy as you listen.

https://artistsforjoy.org/music

Notes

Prelude

xi *I once heard the author Elizabeth Gilbert:* Martha Beck and Rowan Mangan, "Elizabeth Gilbert Gets Bewildered," Bewildered (podcast audio), interview with Elizabeth Gilbert, August 24, 2022, https://marthabeck.com/episodes/elizabeth-gilbert-gets-bewildered/.

xii *I suppose what we all want to know is:* Simon Kyaga, Mikael Landén, Marcus Boman, Christina M. Hultman, Niklas Långström, and Paul Lichtenstein, "Mental Illness, Suicide and Creativity: A 40-Year Prospective Total Population Study," *Journal of Psychiatric Research* 47, no. 1 (2013): 83–90. Semir Zeki, "Art and the Brain," *Journal of Consciousness Studies* 6, no. 6–7 (1999): 76–96.

xii *"'The Mappiness Project,' a study from the early 2000s":* Maura Judkis, "Sex, Exercise and the Arts Make Us Happiest— or So Says an iPhone Survey," *The Washington Post* (online), December 6, 2011, https://www.washingtonpost.com/blogs/arts-post/post/sex-exercise-and-the-arts-make-us-happiest—or-so-says-an-iphone-survey/2011/12/06/gIQAbYVTZO_blog.html.

xii *Numerous studies show how the arts:* Girija Kaimal, Kendra Ray, and Juan Muniz, "Reduction of Cortisol Levels and Participants' Responses Following Art Making," *Art Therapy* 33, no. 2 (1999): 74–80. H. L. Stuckey and J. Nobel, "The Connection between Art, Healing, and Public Health: A Review of Current Literature," *American Journal of Public Health* 100, no. 2 (2010): 254–63. Social Impact of the Arts Project (SIAP), "Culture Builds Community Research Brief: The Power of Arts and Culture in Community Building," Culture Builds Community, February 1, 2002, 3, https://repository.upenn.edu/siap_culture_builds_community/3.

Chapter 1

6   *"Julia Cameron says, 'Discipline is like a battery'":* Julia Cameron, *The Artist's Way: A Spiritual Path to Higher Creativity* (London: Pan, 1995).

8   *The psychologist Carl Jung is often:* Kathrin Asper, *Inner Child in Dreams* (Boston and London: Shambala, 1992).

10   *"as Brené Brown says, 'When perfectionism is driving us'":* Brené Brown, Twitter, "When perfectionism is driving us, shame is always riding shotgun and fear is the backseat driver," 10:00 a.m., June 13, 2013.

11   *It's a common misconception that perfectionism makes us great:* S. B. Sherry, P. L. Hewitt, D. L. Sherry, G. L. Flett, and A. R. Graham, "Perfectionism Dimensions and Research Productivity in Psychology Professors: Implications for Understanding Perfectionism's (Mal)adaptiveness," *Canadian Journal of Behavioural Science/Revue canadienne des sciences du comportement* 42, no. 4 (2010): 273–83.

15   *The Berlin Wall was more than 110 miles long:* The Editors of Encyclopedia Britannica, "Berlin Wall," *Encyclopedia Britannica,* November 13, 2022, https://www.britannica.com/topic/Berlin-Wall.

Chapter 2

18   *Restriction, binging, excessive exercise:* S. Collins, M. Lotfalian, W. Marx, M. Lane, S. Allender, F. Jacka, and E. Hoare, "Associations between Indicators of Diet Quality and Psychological Distress, Depression and Anxiety in Emerging Adults: Results from a Nationally Representative Observational Sample," *Mental Health & Prevention* 24 (2021): 200220.

21   *In Julia Cameron's book The Artist's Way, a creative recovery guide:* Julia Cameron and Natalie Goldberg, *The Artist's Way: A Spiritual Path to Higher Creativity* (New York: TarcherPerigee, 2016), 126.

21   *Perhaps this is what the quote (often attributed:* This quote is attributed to Chekhov, but I have not been able to find a specific source for it. However, it is consistent with his views on art and life, and it is oft quoted in writings about Chekhov.

24   ***Author Sarah Bessey names the key difference:*** Sarah Bessey, *Miracles and Other Reasonable Things: A Story of Unlearning and Relearning God* (New York: Howard Books/Atria, 2020), 169–70.

30   **Wabi-sabi *can look rustic,:*** Graham Parkes and Adam Loughnane, "Japanese Aesthetics," in *The Stanford Encyclopedia of Philosophy*, ed. Edward N. Zalta, Winter 2018 ed., https://plato.stanford.edu/archives/win2018/entries/japanese-aesthetics.

30   ***In* kintsugi*, the art of repairing cracks in pottery:*** Ernest Kurtz and Katherine Ketcham, *The Spirituality of Imperfection: Storytelling and the Search for Meaning* (New York: Bantam Books, 2002).

Chapter 3

35   ***How we spend our days is, of course, how we spend our lives:*** Annie Dillard, *The Writing Life* (New York: Harper Perennial, 2013), 32.

35   ***"Graham says, 'A single meeting can blow a whole afternoon'":*** Paul Graham, *Maker's Schedule, Manager's Schedule*, paulgraham.com, accessed August 14, 2023, http://www.paulgraham.com/makersschedule.html.

37   ***"Mary Oliver tells us 'Attention is the beginning of devotion'":*** Mary Oliver, "Upstream," in *Devotions* (New York: Penguin Random House, 2016), 10.

39   ***"We 'feed the lake,' as Madeleine L'Engle says":*** Madeleine L'Engle, *Walking on Water: Reflections on Faith and Art* (New York: Convergent Books, 2016), 24.

43   ***JJ or JH,* Jesu Juva *or* Jesu Hilfe*:*** Thomas Braats, "Use of Concerto, J.J. and SDG in Bach's Sacred Works," Bach Cantatas (website), August 20–21, 2007, https://www.bach-cantatas.com/Term/Terms-8.htm.

Chapter 4

47   ***One University of Chicago study says one in ten thousand people:*** Max Witynski, "Perfect Pitch, Explained," University of Chicago News, accessed August 14, 2023, https://news.uchicago.edu/explainer/what-is-perfect-pitch.

48 *In* **Let Your Life Speak,** ***Parker Palmer wrote:*** Parker Palmer, *Let Your Life Speak: Listening for the Voice of Vocation* (San Francisco: Jossey-Bass, 2000), 3.

51 ***A young Pablo Casals, a Catalan cellist prodigy:*** Eric Siblin, *The Cello Suites: J. S. Bach, Pablo Casals, and the Search for a Baroque Masterpiece* (New York: Grove Press, 2011).

53 ***"Julia Cameron instructs readers to write 'three pages'":*** Cameron and Goldberg, *The Artist's Way*, 9–18.

53 ***Storyteller Matthew Dicks recommends writing one sentence:*** Matthew Dicks, "Chapter 3: Homework for Life," in *Storyworthy: Engage, Teach, Persuade, and Change Your Life through the Power of Storytelling* (Novato, CA: New World Library, 2018), 37–58.

56 ***Martha Beck, who first taught me about fractals in her book*** **The Way of Integrity:** Martha Nibley Beck, "Chapter 14," in *The Way of Integrity: Finding the Path to Your True Self* (New York: Penguin Life, 2021), 285–304.

Chapter 5

60 ***Or, for artists, in the words of Julia Cameron:*** Cameron and Goldberg, *The Artist's Way*, 154–58.

61 ***An unlearning, an excavation, a remembering:*** Emily McDowell, "Finding Yourself Card," em&friends.com, accessed August 14, 2023, https://emandfriends.com/products/finding-yourself-card.

64 ***Every block of stone has a statue inside it:*** Charles Clément, *Michelangelo* (Portland, OR: Andesite Press, 2015).

65 ***George Doran put forth the S.M.A.R.T. goals:*** G. T. Doran, "There's a S.M.A.R.T. Way to Write Management's Goals and Objectives," *Management Review* 70, no. 11 (1981): 35–36.

68 ***Like a frame around a painting:*** Erin Manning and Brian Massumi, "Toward a Process Seed Bank: What Research-Creation Can Do," *Journal of the New Media Caucus*, September 30, 2015, http://median.newmediacaucus.org/research-creation-explorations/toward-a-process-seed-bank-what-research-creation-can-do.

70 ***As Emily P. Freeman's book encourages us:*** Emily P. Freeman, *The Next Right Thing: A Simple, Soulful Practice for Making Life Decisions* (Grand Rapids, MI: Revell, 2019).

Chapter 6

85 **Scientists like Anita Howard of Case Western Reserve University:** A. Howard, "Positive and Negative Emotional Attractors and Intentional Change," *Journal of Management Development* 25, no. 7 (2006): 657–70.

85 **"Or as Brené Brown reminds us, 'Belonging is belonging'":** Brené Brown, *The Call to Courage* (Netflix, 2018), https://www.netflix.com/watch/81010166.

85 **Graydin's Start with Heart model begins:** Quinn Simpson and McKenzie Cerri, "The Anatomy: The Foundational Coaching Course Handbook" (Graydin.com, 2022), 47.

89 **After the war, she continued fightin':** Kate Clifford Larson, *Bound for the Promised Land: Harriet Tubman, Portrait of an American Hero* (New York: One World, 2005).

Chapter 7

93 **"Jesus says, 'Who of you wouldn't run'":** *The Holy Bible, New International Version* (Grand Rapids, MI: Zondervan, 1995), 1245.

99 **The veracity of these stories of Picasso has been challenged:** Jennifer Dasal, "A Little Curious #7: A Reintroduction, and Cave Paintings," ArtCurious, March 14, 2022, https://www.artcuriouspodcast.com/artcuriouspodcast/alc7. Paul Bahn, "A Lot of Bull: Pablo Picasso and Ice Age Cave Art," *MUNIBE (Antropologia-Arkeologia)* 57 (2005), http://www.aranzadi.eus/fileadmin/docs/Munibe/200503217223AA.pdf.

100 **They do that thing that art does:** Jonathan Jones, "Did Art Peak 30,000 Years Ago? How Cave Paintings Became My Lockdown Obsession," *The Guardian*, April 23, 2021, https://www.theguardian.com/artanddesign/2021/apr/23/cave-paintings-art-lockdown-obsession-30-000-years-lascaux?mc_cid=2f63892133&mc_eid=1fb6cc70a6.

Chapter 8

106 **I read about one writer, Dheepa R. Maturi:** Dheepa R. Maturi, "Moment by Moment," dheeparmaturi.com, December 10, 2019, https://www.dheeparmaturi.com/post/moment-by-moment.

106 *Julia Cameron, Harriet Lerner, and others:* Harriet Goldhor Lerner, *The Dance of Anger: A Woman's Guide to Changing the Patterns of Intimate Relationships* (New York: Quill, 2001). Cameron and Goldberg, *The Artist's Way*, 142.

113 *That figure skating failure was none other than Vera Wang:* Alison Beard, "Life's Work: An Interview with Vera Wang," *Harvard Business Review*, June 18, 2019, https://hbr.org/2019/07/lifes-work-an-interview-with-vera-wang.

Chapter 9

118 *In her book* Finding Your North Star, *sociologist Martha Beck explores:* Martha Nibley Beck, *Finding Your Own North Star: Claiming the Life You Were Meant to Live* (New York: Three Rivers Press, 2002), 60.

118 *The real people who comprise our Everybody:* Beck, *Finding Your Own North Star*, 61.

120 *And these poisonous playmates (as Julia Cameron calls them):* Cameron and Goldberg, *The Artist's Way*, 42.

124 *Let the right Everybody call you home:* Henri Nouwen, *The Inner Voice of Love: A Journey through Anguish to Freedom* (New York: Doubleday, 1996).

128 *At one moment, King hesitated:* Stevie Chick, "'She Told Martin Luther King: Tell 'Em About the Dream!' The Eternal Life of Gospel Singer Mahalia Jackson," *The Guardian*, May 19, 2022, https://www.theguardian.com/music/2022/may/19/mahalia-jackson-martin-luther-king-al-sharpton.

128 *"Historian Jon Meacham said, 'With a single phrase'"* Jon Meacham, "Martin Luther King Jr: Architect of the 21st Century," *Time*, August 26, 2013, https://content.time.com/time/subscriber/article/0,33009,2149610,00.html.

Chapter 10

138 *There's a Spanish saying,* De la panza sale la danza: Paella Party, "10 Spanish Sayings About Food," paella-party.com, August 5, 2020, https://paella-party.com/10-spanish-sayings-about-food.

139 *"This étude is adapted from 'The Anatomy'":* Quinn Simpson and McKenzie Cerri, *The Anatomy: The Foundational Coaching Course Handbook,* 8th ed. (London: Graydin, 2020), 47.

143 ***Astronaut candidates must also have skills in leadership:*** Brian Dunbar, "Astronaut Requirements," NASA, April 8, 2015, https://www.nasa.gov/audience/forstudents/postsecondary/features/F_Astronaut_Requirements.html.

Introduction to Part III

147 ***And part III, the Recapitulation, returns us:*** Maggie Smith, *You Could Make This Place Beautiful* (New York: Ecco, 2023), 123.

Chapter 11

152 ***Simon Sinek's book,* Start with Why*,:*** Simon Sinek, *Start with Why: How Great Leaders Inspire Everyone to Take Action* (London: Portfolio/Penguin, 2013).

152 ***Rick Warren's international bestseller,* A Purpose Driven Life*:*** Rick Warren, *The Purpose Driven Life: What on Earth Am I Here For?* (Grand Rapids, MI: Zondervan, 2002).

153 ***In a conversation with Kate Bowler, Elizabeth Gilbert:*** Kate Bowler and Elizabeth Gilbert, "Why Your Creativity Matters," KateBowler.com, January 20, 2023, https://katebowler.com/podcasts/why-your-creativity-matters.

156 ***Creativity coach, Eric Maisel has you name:*** Eric Maisel, *Coaching the Artist within: Advice for Writers, Actors, Visual Artists, and Musicians from America's Foremost Creativity Coach* (Novato, CA: New World Library, 2005).

156 ***But to keep it from causing you undue purpose anxiety:*** Kendra Adachi and Emily P. Freeman, *The Lazy Genius Way: Embrace What Matters, Ditch What Doesn't, and Get Stuff Done* (Colorado Springs, CO: Waterbrook Press, 2021), 71.

158 ***The finals of the 2022 FIFA World Cup in Qatar:*** Guinness World Records, "Most Penalty Shoot-Outs at a FIFA World Cup Tournament," Guinness World Records, accessed August 14, 2023, https://www.guinnessworldrecords.com/world-records/730726-most-penalty-shoot-outs-at-a-fifa-world-cup-tournament.

158 ***"Brené Brown says, 'Courage starts with showing up'":*** Brené Brown, *Daring Greatly: How the Courage to Be Vulnerable Transforms the Way We Live, Love, Parent, and Lead* (New York: Avery, 2015), 43.

Chapter 12

164 ***Forgiveness. The ability to forgive oneself:*** Ann Patchett, "The Getaway Car," in *This Is the Story of a Happy Marriage* (New York: HarperCollins, 2013), 29–30.

166 ***He left the rumbles in the recap:*** Scott Burnham, "Schubert and the Sound of Memory," *The Musical Quarterly* 84, no. 4 (2000): 655–63.

168 ***I learned from Brené Brown in an interview with Harriet Lerner:*** Brené Brown, "Harriet Lerner and Brené—I'm Sorry: How to Apologize & Why It Matters, Part 1 of 2," brenebrown. com, May 6, 2020, https://brenebrown.com/podcast/harriet-lerner-and-brene-im-sorry-how-to-apologize-why-it-matters-part-1-of-2.

171 ***They want to keep the obstacle:*** "Horsewyse: How Horses See," *Horsewyse Magazine* (2006), https://web.archive.org/web/20161027070011/http://www.horsewyse.com.au/howhorsessee.html.

Chapter 13

173 ***When you get to a place where you understand:*** Brene Brown, "Being Vulnerable About Vulnerability," TED blog, March 16, 2012, https://blog.ted.com/being-vulnerable-about-vulnerability-qa-with-brene-brown/comment-page-2/.

176 ***Studies show that many of us:*** Dena Bravata, Divya Madhusudhan, Michael Boroff, and Kevin Cokley, "Commentary: Prevalence, Predictors, and Treatment of Imposter Syndrome: A Systematic Review," *Journal of Mental Health & Clinical Psychology* 4, no. 3 (2020): 12–16.

177 ***She says, 'We become more courageous by doing courageous acts':*** Brown, *The Gifts of Imperfection*, 7.

183 ***In fact, the word photograph comes from:*** Kristin Farr, "Analyzing the Elements of Art: Four Ways to Think About Value," *New York Times*, January 3, 2018, https://www.nytimes.com/2018/01/03/learning/lesson-plans/analyzing-the-elements-of-art-four-ways-to-think-about-value.html.

Chapter 14

189 *I imagine one of the reasons people cling to their hate:* James Baldwin and Edward P. Jones, *Notes of a Native Son* (Boston: Beacon Press, 2012), 101.

191 *One of my favorite authors, Rachel Held Evans:* Rachel Held Evans and Jeff Chu, *Wholehearted Faith* (San Francisco: HarperOne, 2021), xviii.

192 *But, as Viriginia Woolf wrote, we must not forget:* Virginia Woolf, *The Diary of Virginia Woolf*, ed. Anne Olivier Bell, 5 vols. (New York: Harcourt Brace Jovanovich, 1977–85), vol. 2, 48.

195 *To look outward into space is to peer into the past:* Dennis Overbye, Joshua Sokol, and Kenneth Change, "Webb Telescope Reveals a New Vision of an Ancient Universe," *New York Times*, July 12, 2022.

Chapter 15

197 *The human soul doesn't want to be advised:* Parker J. Palmer, "My Misgivings About Advice," onbeing.org, April 27, 2016, https://onbeing.org/blog/the-gift-of-presence-the-perils-of-advice/.

200 *"Ambassadors promise 'to defend the constitution'":* Colin Powell, "US State Department Archive, Swearing-In New Class of Foreign Service Officers," US Department of State, February 15, 2001, https://2001-2009.state.gov/secretary/former/powell/remarks/2001/588.htm.

202 *"I will find time for play, 'fill the form'":* Cameron and Goldberg, *The Artist's Way*, 140.

202 *I will tell the truth, lean into vulnerability:* Evans and Chu, *Wholehearted Faith*, xvi.

202 *I will be direct about my needs and desires:* Brené Brown, "Clear Is Kind: Unclear Is Unkind," brenebrown.com, October 15, 2018, https://brenebrown.com/articles/2018/10/15/clear-is-kind-unclear-is-unkind.

203 *"Or as C. S. Lewis puts it, 'If I find in myself'":* C. S. Lewis, *Mere Christianity: A Revised and Amplified Edition with a New Introduction of the Three Books: Broadcast Talks* (New York: HarperOne, 1980), 136–37.

205 *As you witness others' oaths, remember Parker Palmer's words:*
Palmer, "My Misgivings About Advice."

207 *One theory is magnetoreception:* Lisa Rolls, "Turtle Teaser: Fast
Facts About Some of the World's Most Ancient Species," UNEP,
June 14, 2017, https://www.unep.org/news-and-stories/story/
turtle-teaser-fast-facts-about-some-worlds-most-ancient-species.

Bonus

213 *They believe that new mothers need just as much care:*
Irina Gonzalez, "Cuarentena: A Latin American Postpartum
Tradition," BabyCenter.com, March 9, 2022, https://www.
babycenter.com/baby/postpartum-health/bringing-back-the-
hispanic-tradition-of-cuarentena-after-chi_10346386.

Creative Recovery Community Guide

221 *The following ideas are a conglomeration of all I have learned:*
Maxine Greene and William Ayers, *Variations on a Blue Guitar:
The Lincoln Center Institute Lectures on Aesthetic Education* (New
York: Teachers College Press, 2018).

221 *Graydin deems asking 'why' to be ineffective:* Simpson and
Cerri, *The Anatomy*, 32.

Index

development, defined, 73
devotion, 36–37, 38–41, 151–52
Dick, Matthew, 53
Dillard, Annie, 34–35
disappointing people, 122–23. *See also* feedback
discipline, 38–41. *See also* practice
disordered eating, 18–20, 22
Doran, George, 65
draw from life concept, 33–34
dreaming
    C.R.A.F.T. goals for, 65–71
    digging for, 63–64
    Five True Things for, 72
    Karl's story regarding, 57–58
    parenting and, 61–62
    self-coaching questions for, 64
    tantrums and, 60–63
    well-crafted goal étude for,
      64–71
drug use, 29

E

ear-training, 46–48
eating/eating disorder, 18–20, 22–23,
    131–32, 135–36
ego, satisfying, 172–74
Elizabeth II (Queen), 104–5
Elle, story of, 195–96, 197–98
Emmie, story of, 147–48, 152–53
Emotional Intelligence, 85
energy management, 34–36
enough, being
    abundance and, 133–34
    body image and, 20, 123–24
    concept of, 93–94
    lies regarding, 104, 189
    overview of, 93–94
    perfectionism and, 10
    truth of, 95
    worthiness and, 181
Estevez, Azucena, 211
étude

build a creative devotion routine,
    41–43
checking in with yourself, 26–27
create a ritual to process grief, 106
create a smile file, 126–27
la Cuarentena - a ritual for being
    done, 213
"Dear Me" letter, 112
defined, xviii
"if onlys" and the information
    they give, 179–81
lens shifting, 137–40
listen to your life, 53–54
name your creative impulse
    metaphor, 192–93
naming Everybody, 125–26
the one, 97–98
retrospective map reading,
    108–9
self-forgiveness list, 168
self-portrait, 84–89
well-crafted goal, 64–71
word-mosaic, 14–15
your artist's oath, 203–4
your "Why (for now)," 154–56
Everybody concept, 118–19, 121–22,
    124, 125–26
exposition, defined, 1
expression, xii, 12

F

failure
    congratulations regarding, 112
    "Dear Me" letter étude for, 112
    Five True Things for, 114
    identity and, 110–11
    map, 106–7, 108–9
    personal contributions to, 107
    personal story regarding, 102–3
    rebounding from, 103–5
    retrospective map reading étude
      for, 108–9
    Sara's story regarding, 101–2